11+
VERBAL REASONING
PRACTICE TEST PAPERS
1, 2 & 3

MULTIPLE-CHOICE
&
STANDARD FORMAT
ANSWERS

11+ Essentials Series

Years 5 - 6

Ages 10 - 11

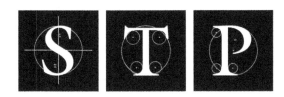

ABOUT THIS BOOK & HOW TO USE IT:

• This book contains **3 <u>full</u> 11+ Verbal Reasoning Practice Test Papers** aimed at candidates **aged 10-11** preparing for the **11+** and other **secondary school entrance exams** containing the **verbal reasoning** element.

• Each Practice Test Paper consists of **80 unrepeated questions** that are **representative** of the types of questions used in **actual exams** set by the **GL board**, which are frequently used by schools.

• Candidates may use one of two means to answer these Practice Test Papers:
   • They may fill their **standard answers** in **by hand** in this book in the spaces provided.
   • Alternatively, they may use the <u>free interactive online</u> **multiple-choice answer pages** for all three Practice Test Papers on our website: www.swottotspublishing.com/online-answer-pages-11plus-verbal-reasoning-multiple-choice-practice-test-papers-collection. These pages also generate **instant test reports** with the candidate's **overall score** out of 80, **score percentage**, and **breakdowns of their performance** (i.e. how they answered each question).

• **Complete answers** for all three Practice Test Papers are included.

• **Complete detailed explanations** showing *why* the correct solutions *are* the correct solutions for all the answers are also included.

• Please note that all the questions in these Practice Test Papers have only **one correct answer**. However, with certain question types, it is possible for candidates to arrive at the correct answer **via routes of reasoning** other than those set out in the explanations.

• A **Glossary** of hard words used in the tests is provided at the end of the book.

• Ensure your child is in a quiet environment when they attempt these Practice Test Papers.
• Use the Practice Test Papers in this book to identify the areas where your child excels and those which they find challenging.
• As these Practice Test Papers become progressively harder, we recommend that they are worked through in order.

CONTENTS

WHAT TO DO BEFORE, WHILE & AFTER
COMPLETING YOUR VERBAL REASONING PRACTICE TEST PAPERS

BEFORE you attempt a Practice Test Paper

- Decide which answer format you want to use.
- **DO NOT** look at either the questions or the multiple-choice online answer pages (if you are using them) **before** you start doing the Practice Test Paper.

WHILE you do a Practice Test Paper

- Work as quickly and as carefully as you can to finish all 80 questions in 50 minutes.
- If you come across a question that you cannot answer quickly, leave it and go back to it at the end if you have time.
- Remember that it **sometimes helps to work things out in writing in rough**, rather than trying to do it all in your head.
- Make sure you provide an answer for **ALL** the questions, even if you are unsure or are simply making an educated guess!

AFTER you finish a Practice Test Paper

- Using the **Answers** section of this book, mark your answers with your parent.
- You can also mark them on your own – just make sure you're being honest with yourself.
- Have another go at the questions you have got wrong, or couldn't do.
- Go through the relevant sections of the **Explanations** that are in this book. You can do this with your parent, or on your own if you wish.

& FINALLY...

Don't be discouraged if you make mistakes.
Remember: it is by making mistakes that we learn.
Also, once you have mastered how to answer the different types of verbal reasoning questions, the best thing you can do to prepare for your exams is to practise, practise, practise – and then practise some more.
The more practice you have, the faster and more accurate you will become.

Last, but not least...

Good luck!

This is a **50 minute test**. Work as quickly, but as accurately, as you can.

Remember: you can also use our ***free online multiple-choice answer pages*** and receive an instant test report when you have finished that provides your overall score out of 80, your score percentage, and a breakdown of how you answered each question.

Simply go to the following page on our website: www.swottotspublishing.com/online-answer-pages-11plus-verbal-reasoning-multiple-choice-practice-test-paper-01

For each of the following, find the **letter** that completes both sets of letter clusters to make two proper words.

Example: *jo ( ) ag   crum ( ) low*   **_b_**

---

1.   gri ( )   ag   ki   ( )   ymph   _____

2.   clas ( )   in   ti   ( )   en   _____

3.   rus ( )   ake   ric ( )   it   _____

4.   ja   ( )   esh   cra ( )   ilk   _____

5.   lor ( )   ig   fin ( )   elve   _____

In each of the following, find **one letter** which can be removed from the first word and added to the second word to make two new proper words.

Example: *SCALE   ALL*   **_C_**

---

6.   DREAM   IN   _____

7.   CAST   AND   _____

8.   BLANK   COVER   _____

9.   BOY   MEN   _____

10. BEAT   PURE   _____

Find the **three-letter word** that completes each of the words in capitals so that every sentence makes sense.

*Example: The cobbler MED my shoe.   **END***

11.   The dragon was a **FSOME** creature.   _____

12.   Celia **CLED** her mother's hand tightly.   _____

13.   All the students **ICKED** the day the results came out.   _____

14.   The brave shepherd offered himself up as a **SACRIF**.   _____

15.   The **ELEOR** has broken down again.   _____

Three of the words in each of the following lists are related in some way. For each question, find the **two words** which do not belong.

*Example: leg   arm   **heart**   hand   **lungs***

16.   morning   breakfast   twilight   lunch   night

17.   the   of   to   an   a

18.   fast   speed   quick   rapid   race

19.   snapdragon   ash   daffodil   elm   peony

20.   confute   conform   obey   comply   collage

In each of the following, find the **two words** – one from the first group and one from the second group – which make a proper new word when combined.

*Example: (**bit** part bite)   (ton **ten** tan)*

21.   (sum   some   sun)   (thin   thing   think)

22.   (ball   bell   bull)   (owed   owes   own)

23.   (par   per   pore)   (sun   den   don)

24.   (poor   sick   ill)   (lea   river   bed)

25.   (for   fur   four)   (age   rage   ire)

In the questions below, find the **pair of letters** that most sensibly completes the analogy. Use the alphabet to help you.

Example: **AB** is to **FG** as **QR** is to (UV **VW** WX VU UX).

A B C D E F G H I J K L M N O P Q R S T U V W X Y Z

26. **JT** is to **QG** as **OD** is to (LW MW LM WL MN).

27. **DC** is to **WV** as **KP** is to (DI PK DE DC EC).

28. **FU** is to **AZ** as **QJ** is to (JQ KJ LO LM OL).   *skip*

29. **MI** is to **JK** as **YB** is to (UV ZB VD DV BZ).

30. **VS** is to **SU** as **BX** is to (WX XY YX ZA YZ).

In the following questions, the numbers in each group are related in the same way. Find the **missing number** in the third group.

Example: 9 (10) 1   4 (7) 3   8 (?) 8   __16__

31.   5 (16) 9   4 (15) 9   3 (?) 8   _____

32.   4 (12) 2   3 (19) 5   2 (?) 6   _____   *skip*

33.   12 (14) 3   7 (10) 2   8 (?) 2   _____

34.   2 (16) 10   3 (23) 9   7 (?) 8   _____

35.   20 (3) 14   11 (1) 9   15 (?) 7   _____

The number codes for three of the four following words are listed randomly below. Work out the **code** to answer the questions.

RAID   DRAW   WORD   DRAM   *skip*
4261   7524   2694

36.   Find the code for **DRAM**.   _____

37.   Find the code for **WARD**.   _____

38.   What does the code **1694** stand for?   _____

The number codes for three of the four following words are listed randomly below. Work out the **code** to answer the questions.

ONLY   LINE   HILT   LONE

2463   8769   6475

39.   Find the code for **ONLY**.   _____

40.   What does the code **8469** stand for?   _____

41.   What does the code **3846** stand for?   _____

Carefully read the following information, then **answer the question** below.

42.   Gemma's mother has two sisters who both have two children. Her father has three brothers, but only one of them has any children. Gemma herself has one brother and two sisters.

If all these statements are true, only one of the sentences below **cannot be true**. Which one?

A.   Gemma has five aunts.   ☐

B.   Gemma's parents have four children.   ☐

C.   Gemma only has four cousins.   ☐

D.   Gemma's father has no sisters.   ☐

E.   Gemma is eleven years old.   ☐

For each of the questions below, find a **word** that completes the third pair of words so that it follows the same pattern as the first two pairs.

Example: site sit   cute cut   pipe ?   __pip__

43.   indigo go   nearby by   fruit ?   _____

44.   relate real   dilate dial   melange ?   _____

45. calf lace   rack care   daft ?   _____

46. attire tire   entice nice   impale ?   _____

47. little it   cattle at   stormy ?   _____

For the following, find the **word** from the list of words given that has a similar meaning to the words in both pairs of brackets.

Example: *(shop market) (save reserve)*   buy   keep   <u>**store**</u>   gather   collect

---

48. (request plea) (attraction interest)   appeal   application   charm   petition   allure

49. (stand kiosk) (delay postpone)   defer   stall   hedge   booth   coop

50. (nurse nurture) (lean incline)   treat   nourish   bend   tend   curve

51. (staff rod) (beat hit)   cane   crook   stick   bash   box

52. (reckless impulsive) (rapid speedy)   imprudent   hasty   quick   brisk   fast

---

In the next questions, choose **two words**, one from each set of brackets, which complete the sentence in the most sensible way.

Example: **Meat** is to (**<u>food</u>** animal pet) as **juice** is to (orange **<u>drink</u>** sugary).

---

53. **Here** is to (hear there present) as **this** is to (these those that).

54. **Italy** is to (Sofia Lisbon Rome) as **Germany** is to (Berlin Frankfurt Hamburg).

55. **Current** is to (electricity now currant) as **feet** is to (shoes hooves feat).

56. **Canary** is to (yellow wine island) as **crow** is to (croak black cockerel).

57. **Flat** is to (pancake level apartment) as **light** is to (lamp heavy feather).

58. **Litter** is to (litre puppies dogs) as **pack** is to (wolves park monkeys).

59. **Hit** is to (knock success miss) as **stop** is to (master go red).

In the questions below, each letter stands for a number. Work out the **letter solution** to each sum.

Example: *A = 5, B = 3, C = 2, D = 6, E = 11* $A \times B - C^2 \times C \div E =$ <u>***C***</u>

---

60. A = 8, B = 12, C = 16, D = 4, E = 6 $C \div A \times B \div E =$ _____

61.   A = 2, B = 4, C = 6, D = 8 $3B \div C = $ _____

62.   A = 1, B = 3, C = 5, D = 6, E = 7 $B(A + C) \div D = $ _____

63.   A = 3, B = 4, C = 6, D = 12, E = 18 $E - C \div B + A = $ _____

64.   A = 2, B = 4, C = 5, D = 6, E = 9 $(C + D + E) - 2E = $ _____

In the following, each question uses a different code. Work out the **code** in order to answer the question. Use the alphabet to help you.

Example: *If the code for CAB is GEF, what is the code for POTTER?*   *TSXXIV*

A B C D E F G H I J K L M N O P Q R S T U V W X Y Z

65.   If the code for **MONEY** is **NQQID**, what is the code for **CANDY**?   _____

66.   If the code for **STREET** is **UVTGGV**, what is the code for **AVENUE**?   _____

67.   If the code for **WAXY** is **DZCB**, what is the code for **FAIN**?   _____

68.   If the code for **SHORE** is **FQPNC**, what does **QPNFC** stand for?   _____

69.   If the code for **BUTCHER** is **YFGXSVI**, what is the code for **STATION**?   _____

Carefully read the following information, then **answer the question** below.

---

70.   Anne, Sarah, Ahmed, Ali, and Michel all went to a bookshop on Saturday. Everyone except Anne bought a science fiction novel. Anne, Sarah, and Michel all chose a book about dinosaurs. They all bought the latest Wimpy Kid book, apart from Anne. Only Ahmed decided to purchase a book on aeroplanes.

Who bought the **fewest books**?   _____

For the following, find the **number** that continues each sequence in the best way.

Example: *2,   4,   6,   8,   10,   **12***

---

71.   1, 4, 7, 10, 13, _____

72.   4, 7, 5, 6, 6, _____

      +3, -2, +1, -0

73. 1, 2, 3, 5, 8, _____

74. 7, 3, 6, 5, 5, _____

75. 36, 25, 16, 9, _____

In the next questions, the words in the second set follow the same pattern as the words in the first set. Work out the rule to find the **missing word** to complete the second set.

Example: *pour (pod) bud*   *leaf (?) sit*   <u>**let**</u>

76.   name (mat) till   hole (?) game   _____

77.   omen (mode) idle   mend (?) list   _____

78.   bang (ring) irate   part (?) offer   _____

79.   lame (meat) outing   wave (?) allows   _____

80.   book (tool) tell   maze (?) lacy   _____

TOTAL SCORE: _____ / 80

END OF PRACTICE TEST PAPER 1

PRACTICE TEST PAPER 2

This is a **50 minute test**. Work as quickly, but as accurately, as you can.

Remember: you can also use our **_free online multiple-choice answer pages_** and receive an instant test report when you have finished that provides your overall score out of 80, your score percentage, and a breakdown of how you answered each question.

Simply go to the following page on our website: www.swottotspublishing.com/online-answer-pages-11plus-verbal-reasoning-multiple-choice-practice-test-paper-02

In the questions below, each letter stands for a number. Work out the **letter solution** to each sum.

Example: $A = 5, B = 3, C = 2, D = 6, E = 11$ $A \times B - C^2 \times C \div E =$ __*C*__

---

1. $A = 3, B = 4, C = 6, D = 12, E = 18$ $C \div A \times D \div B =$ _____

2. $A = 2, B = 4, C = 5, D = 7, E = 0$ $3C - (D + B) =$ _____

3. $A = 3, B = 4, C = 18, D = 6, E = 12$ $E \times D \div B \div A =$ _____

4. $A = 1, B = 3, C = 5, D = 8$ $2A \times D - BC =$ _____

5. $A = 4, B = 5, C = 6, D = 7$ $(B^2 - D) + 3A \div C =$ _____

For each of the questions below, find a **word** that completes the third pair of words so that it follows the same pattern as the first two pairs.

Example: site   sit   cute   cut   pipe   ?   __**pip**__

---

6.   totters   tort   seating   sent   condole   ?   _____

7.   hater   halter   taker   talker   saved   ?   _____

8.   monsoon   moon   pharmacy   pacy   deliberate   ?   _____

9.   spinner   nip   staple   pat   swollen   ?   _____

10.   potter   poet   slider   sled   pommel   ?   _____

For the following, find the **word** from the list of words given that has a similar meaning to the words in both pairs of brackets.

Example: *(shop market) (save reserve)* buy keep **store** gather collect

11. (arrow bolt) (dash flit)   shaft flight sprint scurry dart

12. (wealthy affluent) (creamy tasty)   rich heavy delicious prosperous fatty

13. (journey tour) (stumble tumble)   slip trip totter voyage spin

14. (ascend escalate) (rebel revolt)   soar increase rise riot mutiny

15. (occasionally sporadically) (regularly cyclically)   intermittently repeatedly routinely periodically infrequently

---

In the questions below, find the **pair of letters** that most sensibly completes the analogy. Use the alphabet to help you.

Example: **AB** is to **FG** as **QR** is to (UV **VW** WX VU UX).

A B C D E F G H I J K L M N O P Q R S T U V W X Y Z

16. **AN** is to **WT** as **LN** is to (GT IT HT HU HS).

17. **SH** is to **NM** as **WD** is to (HS QJ IR RI DW).

18. **MB** is to **QV** as **BM** is to (FG GF VQ EF EG).

19. **HK** is to **PS** as **GI** is to (TR RJ NM MN RT).

20. **RI** is to **VE** as **JQ** is to (MN PK LO NM EV).

In each sentence below, a **four-letter word** is hidden at the end of one word and the start of the next. Find the hidden word.

Example: "I alway**s wan**ted to be a doctor," Sita said.   __*swan*__

21. Jim stared as the floating oval elongated.   _____

22. The alligator's vicious jaws opened wide.   _____

23. The Ancient Egyptians made linen garments.   _____

24. Albion is a wonderful, mystical land.   _____

25.   Local councils are abolishing parking fines.   _____

Carefully read the following information, then **answer the question** below.

26.   At their school sports day five children took part in the egg and spoon race. Ella finished in front of Oscar, but behind Arthur. Fiona led all the way, but dropped her egg just before the finishing line. Lamia completed the race in 33 seconds, just 3 seconds faster than Ella. Oscar was 4 seconds slower than Lamia and 5 seconds behind the winner.

If all these statements are true, only one of the sentences below **must be true**. Which one?

   A.   Arthur completed the race in 34 seconds.   ☐

   B.   Lamia finished in second place.   ☐

   C.   Oscar came third.   ☐

   D.   Fiona tripped over.   ☐

   E.   Ella was disqualified.   ☐

In the following questions, the numbers in each group are related in the same way. Find the **missing number** in the third group.

Example: 9 (10) 1   4 (7) 3   8 (?) 8   **16**

27.   21 (72) 3   9 (30) 1   22 (?) 3   _____

28.   70 (4) 42   49 (4) 21   63 (?) 14   _____

29.   36 (14) 9   25 (12) 4   64 (?) 49   _____

30.   39 (36) 5   67 (80) 21   52 (?) 16   _____

31.   5 (32) 1   4 (16) 2   7 (?) 2   _____

In each of the following, find **one letter** which can be removed from the first word and added to the second word to make two new proper words.

Example: SCALE   ALL   _C_

32.   OWED   ROT   _____

33.   CLAMP   HOPED   _____

34.   WORE   ANGER   _____

35.   FRANK   SOT   _____

36.   EMERGE   LAD   _____

For each of the following questions, find the **term** that continues the sequence in the most logical way. Use the alphabet to help you.

Example: 2K,   3M,   4O,   5Q,   **6S**

A B C D E F G H I J K L M N O P Q R S T U V W X Y Z

37.   JJ, NK, MF, QG, PB, _____

38.   NDX, PHR, RLL, TPF, _____

39.   C, I, I, K, N, M, R, _____

40.   25C, 21F, 17I, 13L, _____

41.   12Tt, 10Ww, 7Ux, 5Xa, _____

42.   D19, F18, E16, G13, _____

43.   G, A, W, U, U, _____

In the following, find the **two words** – one from each set – which are the closest in meaning.

Example: (**sound** healthy ill)   (**noise** quiet whisper)

44.   (nail finger digit)   (eleven hammer tack)

45.   (choice choose option)   (best opinion select)

46.   (evenly straight line)   (coolly jagged icicle)

47. (mistake   forsake   keepsake)   (moment   memento   pimento)

48. (fireside   beside   bedside)   (warmth   adjust   adjacent)

In the next questions, the words in the second set follow the same pattern as the words in the first set. Work out the rule to find the **missing word** to complete the second set.

Example: pour (pod) bud   leaf (?) sit   __*let*__

---

49.   apples (paws) sown   inkier (?) done   _____

50.   smell (mile) pink   stems (?) gang   _____

51.   dame (mark) fork   rise (?) bare   _____

52.   easy (year) rare   anew (?) dirt   _____

53.   supper (push) harm   laughs (?) ends   _____

54.   coal (core) area   jump (?) stem   _____

55.   talk (rank) ring   bled (?) poor   _____

Carefully read the following information, then **answer the questions** below.

56.   All the children who attend the breakfast club are given fruit juice to drink. Josh's favourites are orange, cranberry, and fruit cocktail, but he sometimes chooses grapefruit. Neville and Mike prefer blueberry and grapefruit, but they also like cranberry. Sheila only really likes orange, but will accept fruit cocktail if there is no orange left. George never drinks grapefruit juice, but always has either orange or blueberry.

Which is the **least popular** fruit juice?   _____

57.   Bertrand, Francois, Aisha, Alaa, and Gerhardt are all tourists visiting London. Bertrand, Francois, and Gerhardt all go on the London Eye. None of them visit the British Museum apart from Francois. All of them go and watch the Changing the Guard ceremony at Buckingham Palace except Alaa. They all see the waxwork models at Madame Tussaud's with the exception of Bertrand and Francois. Gerhardt and Alaa fit in a visit to the National Gallery as well.

Who manages to visit the **most attractions**?   _____

The number codes for three of the four following words are listed randomly below Work out the **code** to answer the questions.

SING   GONE   DINE   SONG

8457   3957   2953

58.   Find the code for **GONE**.   _____

59.   Find the code for **NINE**.   _____

60.   What does the code **2995** stand for?   _____

61.   What does the code **5927** stand for?   _____

The number codes for three of the four following words are listed randomly below. Work out the **code** to answer the questions.

RUNE   DARN   TUNE   RUDE

7469   3489   6278

62.   Find the code for **RUNE**.   _____

63.   Find the code for **NEAR**.   _____

64.   What does the code **7483** stand for?   _____

65.   What does the code **6279** stand for?   _____

In the next questions, find the **missing number** which completes the sum correctly.

Example: $17 - 3 \div 2 = 6 \times 6 - 8 \div (?)$ __4__

66. $7 \times 7 - 9 \div 4 = 31 - 4 \div 9 + (?)$ _____

67. $17 - 5 \times 2 \div 8 = 6 \times 8 \div 12 - (?)$ _____

68. $2 + 14 \div 4 + 8 = 18 \times 2 \div 9 + (?)$ _____

69. $81 \div 3 - 4 \times 2 = 34 \div 2 - 2 \times 3 + (?)$ _____

70. $21 + 3 - 9 \div 3 = 39 - 14 + 10 \div (?)$ _____

Find the **three-letter word** that completes each of the words in capitals so that every sentence makes sense.

Example: The cobbler MED my shoe. ___**END**___

71. The orange was so rotten that it was full of **MAGS**. _____

72. When his brother took his toy away from him, Luke **BAW** loudly. _____

73. The young girl was wearing a pink **CARAN**. _____

74. Sam's behaviour was utterly **UNACCEPLE**. _____

75. My grandmother left me an **EXSIVE** ring in her will. _____

√

For the questions below, find the **two words** – one from each set – which are the most opposite in meaning.

Example: (funny ***happy*** sad) (sunken ***depressed*** bent)

76. (whisper   sigh   loud)   (noise   quiet   aside)

77. (beside   over   furbelow)   (above   bury   below)

78. (fact   science   true)   (novel   story   fiction)

79. (wiry   coyly   bronze)   (shyly   brazenly   coil)

80. (spectacles   see   blind)   (bat   sighted   eye)

TOTAL SCORE: _____ / 80

END OF PRACTICE TEST PAPER 2

PRACTICE TEST PAPER 3

This is a **50 minute test**. Work as quickly, but as accurately, as you can.

Remember: you can also use our *__free online multiple-choice answer pages__* and receive an instant test report when you have finished that provides your overall score out of 80, your score percentage, and a breakdown of how you answered each question.

Simply go to the following page on our website: www.swottotspublishing.com/online-answer-pages-11plus-verbal-reasoning-multiple-choice-practice-test-paper-03

For the following, find the **word** from the list of words given that has a similar meaning to the words in both pairs of brackets.

Example: (shop market) (save reserve)   buy   keep   __store__   gather   collect

---

1.   (disgusting foul) (class grade)   revolting offensive putrid rank sort

2.   (overlook neglect) (mourn lament)   miss forget grieve ignore omit

3.   (healthy sound) (spring fount)   reservoir source well strong robust

4.   (stew ferment) (develop gather)   steep boil evolve grow brew

5.   (wallop cuff) (success winner)   triumph bash buffet hit box

---

Carefully read the following information, then **answer the question** below.

---

6.   Sally, Barbara, Monica, Sonia and Ola all love music and play five different instruments between them. Four of them play the violin. Sally plays the flute, but doesn't play the piano. Barbara can play neither the flute, the violin nor the piano. Monica and Sonia can both play the harp and the piano. Sally, Monica, Barbara and Ola are all good guitarists.

Who plays the **least number** of musical instruments?   _____

For the following, find the **number** that continues each sequence in the best way.

Example: 2,   4,   6,   8,   10,   **12**

7.   1,   2,   3,   4,   6,   7,   10,   11,   _____

8.   73,   62,   53,   46,   41,   _____

9.   81,   64,   49,   36,   _____

10.   128,   120,   32,   124,   8,   128,   _____

11.   10,   6,   8,   6,   7,   6,   7,   6,   _____

For each of the questions below, find a **word** that completes the third pair of words so that it follows the same pattern as the first two pairs.

Example: site   sit   cute   cut   pipe   ?   **pip**

12.   shame   mesh   arcane   near   infra   ?   _____

13.   tile   tall   bile   ball   mile   ?   _____

14.   preen   pen   deaden   den   maiden   ?   _____

15.   sledging   leg   swingers   wig   stagnant   ?   _____

16.   tamarind   mat   taste   sat   debate   ?   _____

In the following, each question uses a different code. Work out the **code** in order to answer the question. Use the alphabet to help you.

Example: If the code for **CAB** is **GEF**, what is the code for **POTTER**?   **TSXXIV**

A B C D E F G H I J K L M N O P Q R S T U V W X Y Z

17.   If the code for **FRIEND** is **CPHEOF**, what does **JGMCFF** stand for?   _____

18.   If the code for **DRESS** is **ETHWX**, what does **TMLVY** stand for?   _____

19.   If the code for **RESIN** is **RJSNN**, what is the code for **PLATE**?   _____

20.   If the code for **MILK** is **NROP**, what is the code for **FADED**?   _____

21.   If the code for **WOLF** is **ACNK**, what is the code for **FOWL**?   _____

For each of the following, find the **letter** that completes both sets of letter clusters to make two proper words.

Example: jo ( ) ag   crum ( ) low   **_b_**

22.   albu ( ) aroon   tote ( ) itten   _____

23.   live ( ) evel   chai ( ) obin   _____

24.   ditt ( ) yster   tang ( ) ctave   _____

25.   shru ( ) ruel   stin ( ) ouge   _____

26.   asses ( ) cythe   stres ( ) taunch   _____

Three of the words in each of the following lists are related in some way. For each question, find the **two words** which do not belong.

Example: leg   arm   **heart**   hand   **lungs**

27.   drink   chew   sip   bite   gulp

28.   minority   mass   majority   bulk   handful

29.   peel   wing   leg   fur   skin

30.   over   under   and   below   so

31.   dragon   witch   sorcerer   gryphon   warlock

The number codes for three of the four following words are listed randomly below. Work out the **code** to answer the questions.

GRAB   BOAR   ROBE   BADE

4512   7654   4356

32.   Find the code for **BOAR**.   _____

33.   Find the code for **BARE**.   _____

34.   What does the code **6572** stand for?   _____

35.   What does the code **7362** stand for?   _____

Each set of symbols stands for one of the words listed below. **Match** the sets of symbols to the correct words.

TASTE   SEATS   STEMS   STEAM   ASTIR

36.   + * ? - $ _____

37.   * ? £ ! *   _____

38.   ? + * ? £   _____

39.   * ? £ + !   _____

Carefully read the following information, then **answer the question** below.

40.   Five children all live less than a mile away from their school. It takes Lucy 10 minutes to go there on foot. Harris and Calum arrive there by bike before Jimmy every day. Tilly's mum takes her in the car and gets her there 4 minutes faster than Lucy. Jimmy uses his scooter and arrives in less than 10 minutes.

If all these statements are true, only one of the sentences below **must be true**. Which one?

A.   Harris and Calum are brothers.   ☐

B.   Lucy is always later than Tilly.   ☐

C.   Jimmy lives closer to the school than Tilly.   ☐

D.   Calum always arrives before Jimmy.   ☐

E.   Lucy always walks to school.   ☐

In the questions below, each letter stands for a number. Work out the **letter solution** to each sum.

Example: *A = 5, B = 3, C = 2, D = 6, E = 11* $A \times B - C^2 \times C \div E =$ __C__

41.   A = 8, B = 12, C = 16, D = 4, E = 6 $A \times B \div E - D =$ _____

42.   A = 3,   B = 4,   C = 6,   D = 12,   E = 18 $E - D \times C \div A = $ _____

43.   A = 3,   B = 4,   C = 6,   D = 8 $(C^2 - B) \div D = $ _____

44.   A = 3,   B = 4,   C = 18,   D = 6,   E = 12 $C \times D \div E + A = $ _____

45.   A = 3,   B = 4,   C = 5,   D = 6 $(4B + BC) \div D = $ _____

46.   A = 1,   B = 2,   C = 3,   D = 4 $5(B + C) - 6D = $ _____

Find the **three-letter word** that completes each of the words in capitals so that every sentence makes sense.

Example: *The cobbler MED my shoe.*   __**END**__

---

47.   The king entered the hall amidst a **FANE** of trumpets.   _____

48.   Pleased with himself, Tony **SGERED** into the room.   _____

49.   The wall was covered with colourful **GRAFI**.   _____

50.   "I have a **RANT** for your arrest!" yelled the policeman.   _____

51.   As the weather was nice, we had lunch on the **TACE**.   _____

In the next questions, choose **two words**, one from each set of brackets, which complete the sentence in the most sensible way.

Example: **Meat** *is to (**food** animal pet) as* **juice** *is to (orange **drink** sugary).*

---

52.   **Mine** is to (belong   tunnel   gold) as **well** is to (water   health   bucket).

53.   **Lightning** is to (flash   speed   bright) as **thunder** is to (loud   rumble   cloud).

54.   **Fight** is to (combat   battle   flight) as **sight** is to (sigh   slight   seen).

55.   **Bad** is to (worse   worst   terrible) as **good** is to (better   well   healthy).

56.   **Hutch** is to (cage   house   tame) as **burrow** is to (wild   den   lair).

In the following questions, the numbers in each group are related in the same way. Find the **missing number** in the third group.

Example: *9 (10) 1*   *4 (7) 3*   *8 (?) 8*   __**16**__

---

57.   9 (5) 4   16 (9) 25   4 (?) 36   _____

58.   17 (9) 14   20 (36) 14   10 (?) 8   _____

59.   8 (11) 36   16 (9) 20   12 (?) 24   _____

60.   5 (42) 9   13 (78) 13   6 (?) 9   _____

61.   11 (20) 2   3 (19) 7   3 (?) 2   _____

For the questions below, find the **two words** – one from each set – which are the most opposite in meaning.

*Example: (funny **happy** sad)   (sunken **depressed** bent)*

62.   (obese   oboe   oblong)   (shape   thin   tone)

63.   (fakir   fake   fête)   (jig   reel   real)

64.   (pick   sow   reap)   (grain   harvest   wheat)

65.   (heartfelt   false   disingenuous)   (insincere   heartburn   indigestion)

66.   (third   part   behind)   (first   before   prior)

In the next questions, the words in the second set follow the same pattern as the words in the first set. Work out the rule to find the **missing word** to complete the second set.

*Example: pour (pod) bud   leaf (?) sit   **let**__

67.   cello (lock) knight   molar (?) slight   _____

68.   arrow (road) clod   using (?) plug   _____

69.   medium (must) astern   absorb (?) pander   _____

70.   odour (plod) palls   medic (?) helix   _____

71.   upper (pull) calls   anger (?) mater   _____

In the questions below, find the **pair of letters** that most sensibly completes the analogy. Use the alphabet to help you.

Example: **AB** is to **FG** as **QR** is to (UV **VW** WX VU UX).

A B C D E F G H I J K L M N O P Q R S T U V W X Y Z

72.   **AM** is to **DO** as **PT** is to (SW   RV   SU   RU   SV).

73.   **ZY** is to **BA** as **XW** is to (ZY   CD   YZ   DC   YD).

74.   **GC** is to **TX** as **KE** is to (QV   PV   PU   QW   PE).

75.   **GT** is to **EV** as **KP** is to (IQ   JR   HR   IS   IR).

76.   **CM** is to **NX** as **AE** is to (VW   VZ   ZV   XC   CX).

In each of the following, find the **two words** – one from the first group and one from the second group – which make a proper new word when combined.

Example: (**bit** part bite)   (ton **ten** tan)

77.   (bed   bud   bid)   (rack   wreck   rock)

78.   (part   partner   pa)   (snip   ship   shop)

79.   (on   in   at)   (us   we   it)

80.   (hill   mound   col)   (lock   lour   our)

TOTAL SCORE: _____ / 80

END OF PRACTICE TEST PAPER 3

ANSWERS

Pages 26 and 27 provide the answers to Practice Test Papers 1, 2 & 3. The page numbers on the right-hand side of each column indicate where to find each answer's corresponding detailed explanation.

PRACTICE TEST PAPER 1

(1) n	p. 28
(2) p	p. 28
(3) h	p. 28
(4) m	p. 28
(5) d	p. 28
(6) D	p. 28
(7) S	p. 28
(8) L	p. 28
(9) O	p. 28
(10) E	p. 28
(11) EAR	p. 28
(12) ASP	p. 28
(13) PAN	p. 28
(14) ICE	p. 28
(15) VAT	p. 28
(16) breakfast; lunch	p. 28
(17) of; to	p. 28
(18) speed; race	p. 28
(19) ash; elm	p. 28
(20) confute; collage	p. 28
(21) some; thing	p. 28
(22) bell; owed	p. 28
(23) par; don	p. 29
(24) sick; bed	p. 29
(25) for; age	p. 29
(26) LW	p. 29
(27) DI	p. 29
(28) LO	p. 29
(29) VD	p. 29
(30) YZ	p. 29
(31) 13	p. 29
(32) 16	p. 29
(33) 11	p. 29
(34) 52	p. 29
(35) 4	p. 29
(36) 4261	p. 29
(37) 7624	p. 29
(38) MAID	p. 29
(39) 8769	p. 29

(40) OILY	p. 29
(41) TOIL	p. 29
(42) C	p. 29
(43) it	p. 30
(44) meal	p. 30
(45) fade	p. 30
(46) male	p. 30
(47) to	p. 30
(48) appeal	p. 30
(49) stall	p. 30
(50) tend	p. 31
(51) cane	p. 31
(52) hasty	p. 31
(53) there; that	p. 31
(54) Rome; Berlin	p. 31
(55) currant; feat	p. 31
(56) yellow; black	p. 31
(57) pancake; feather	p. 31
(58) puppies; wolves	p. 31
(59) miss; go	p. 31
(60) D	p. 31
(61) A	p. 31
(62) B	p. 31
(63) C	p. 31
(64) A	p. 31
(65) DCQHD	p. 32
(66) CXGPWG	p. 32
(67) UZRM	p. 32
(68) HORSE	p. 32
(69) HGZGRLM	p. 32
(70) Anne	p. 32
(71) 16	p. 32
(72) 5	p. 32
(73) 13	p. 32
(74) 7	p. 32
(75) 4	p. 32
(76) log	p. 32
(77) emit	p. 33
(78) fort	p. 33
(79) veal	p. 33
(80) lazy	p. 33

PRACTICE TEST PAPER 2

(1) C	p. 34
(2) B	p. 34
(3) D	p. 34
(4) A	p. 34
(5) B	p. 34
(6) cold	p. 34
(7) salved	p. 34
(8) date	p. 34
(9) low	p. 35
(10) poem	p. 35
(11) dart	p. 35
(12) rich	p. 35
(13) trip	p. 35
(14) rise	p. 35
(15) periodically	p. 35
(16) HT	p. 35
(17) RI	p. 35
(18) FG	p. 35
(19) RT	p. 35
(20) NM	p. 35
(21) vale	p. 35
(22) heal	p. 35
(23) deli	p. 35
(24) call	p. 35
(25) area	p. 35
(26) B	p. 35
(27) 75	p. 36
(28) 7	p. 36
(29) 20	p. 36
(30) 60	p. 36
(31) 40	p. 36
(32) O	p. 36
(33) P	p. 36
(34) R	p. 36
(35) F	p. 36
(36) E	p. 36
(37) TC	p. 36
(38) VTZ	p. 36

(39) O	p. 37
(40) 9O	p. 37
(41) 2Vb	p. 37
(42) F9	p. 37
(43) W	p. 37
(44) nail; tack	p. 37
(45) choose; select	p. 37
(46) evenly; coolly	p. 37
(47) keepsake; memento	p. 38
(48) beside; adjacent	p. 38
(49) kind	p. 38
(50) tame	p. 38
(51) sire	p. 38
(52) wand	p. 38
(53) gale	p. 38
(54) jute	p. 38
(55) plod	p. 39
(56) fruit cocktail	p. 39
(57) Gerhardt	p. 39
(58) 3957	p. 39
(59) 5457	p. 39
(60) SOON	p. 39
(61) NOSE	p. 39
(62) 7489	p. 39
(63) 8927	p. 40
(64) RUNT	p. 40
(65) DARE	p. 40
(66) 7	p. 40
(67) 1	p. 40
(68) 8	p. 40
(69) 1	p. 40
(70) 7	p. 40
(71) GOT	p. 40
(72) LED	p. 40
(73) DIG	p. 40
(74) TAB	p. 40
(75) PEN	p. 40
(76) loud; quiet	p. 40
(77) over; below	p. 40
(78) fact; fiction	p. 40
(79) coyly; brazenly	p. 40
(80) blind; sighted	p. 41

PRACTICE TEST PAPER 3

(1) rank	p. 42
(2) miss	p. 42
(3) well	p. 42
(4) brew	p. 42
(5) hit	p. 42
(6) Barbara	p. 42
(7) 15	p. 42
(8) 38	p. 42
(9) 25	p. 42
(10) 2	p. 42
(11) 8	p. 43
(12) rain	p. 43
(13) mall	p. 43
(14) men	p. 43
(15) tan	p. 43
(16) bed	p. 43
(17) MINCED	p. 43
(18) SKIRT	p. 43
(19) PQAYE	p. 44
(20) UZWVW	p. 44
(21) KCAN	p. 44
(22) m	p. 44
(23) r	p. 44
(24) o	p. 44
(25) g	p. 44
(26) s	p. 44
(27) chew; bite	p. 44
(28) minority; handful	p. 44
(29) wing; leg	p. 44
(30) and; so	p. 44
(31) dragon; gryphon	p. 44
(32) 4356	p. 44
(33) 4562	p. 44
(34) RAGE	p. 44
(35) GORE	p. 44
(36) ASTIR	p. 44
(37) STEMS	p. 44
(38) TASTE	p. 44
(39) STEAM	p. 44
(40) D	p. 45
(41) B	p. 45
(42) D	p. 45
(43) B	p. 45
(44) E	p. 45

(45) D	p. 45
(46) A	p. 45
(47) FAR	p. 45
(48) WAG	p. 45
(49) FIT	p. 45
(50) WAR	p. 45
(51) ERR	p. 46
(52) gold; water	p. 46
(53) flash; rumble	p. 46
(54) flight; slight	p. 46
(55) worse; better	p. 46
(56) tame; wild	p. 46
(57) 8	p. 46
(58) 4	p. 46
(59) 9	p. 46
(60) 45	p. 46
(61) 4	p. 46
(62) obese; thin	p. 46
(63) fake; real	p. 46
(64) sow; harvest	p. 46
(65) heartfelt; insincere	p. 46
(66) behind; before	p. 46
(67) arms	p. 46
(68) snug	p. 46
(69) bran	p. 47
(70) hide	p. 47
(71) gate	p. 47
(72) SV	p. 47
(73) DC	p. 47
(74) PV	p. 47
(75) IR	p. 47
(76) VZ	p. 47
(77) bed; rock	p. 47
(78) partner; ship	p. 47
(79) on; us	p. 47
(80) col; our	p. 47

PRACTICE TEST PAPER 1: EXPLANATIONS

1. Adding **n** to the given letter clusters results in the following words: **grin nag kin nymph**. The letters b, d, f, g, h, j, l, m, p, r, s, t, and w can be used to complete some, but not all four, of the letter clusters.

2. Adding **p** to the given letter clusters results in the following words: **clasp pin tip pen**. The letters b, d, f, g, h, k, m, n, s, t, w, y, and z can be used to complete some, but not all four, of the letter clusters.

3. Adding **h** to the given letter clusters results in the following words: **rush hake rich hit**. The letters b, c, e, f, k, l, m, n, p, r, s, t, w, y, and z can be used to complete some, but not all four, of the letter clusters.

4. Adding **m** to the given letter clusters results in the following words: **jam mesh cram milk**. The letters b, g, p, r, w, and y can be used to complete some, but not all four, of the letter clusters.

5. Adding **d** to the given letter clusters results in the following words: **lord dig find delve**. The letters b, c, e, f, g, p, r, s, and w can be used to complete some, but not all four, of the letter clusters.

6. By removing **D** from <u>D</u>REAM and adding it to IN, we get the new words: **REAM DIN**. While E can be removed from DREAM to give DRAM, it cannot be added to IN in any way to form a proper word.

7. By removing **S** from CA<u>S</u>T and adding it to AND, we get the new words: **CAT SAND**. No other letters can be removed from CAST to give a proper word.

8. By removing **L** from B<u>L</u>ANK and adding it to COVER, we get the new words: **BANK CLOVER**. While B can be removed from BLANK to give LANK, it cannot be added to COVER in any way to form a proper word.

9. By removing **O** from B<u>O</u>Y and adding it to MEN, we get the new words: **BY OMEN**. No other letters can be removed from BOY to give a proper word.

10. By removing **E** from B<u>E</u>AT and adding it to PURE, we get the new words: **BAT PURE<u>E</u>**. While A can be removed from BEAT to give BET, and B can be removed from BEAT to give EAT, neither A nor B can be added to PURE in any way to make a proper word.

11. The completed word in the sentence should read as follows: The dragon was a **FEAR<u>SOME</u>** creature. Although the three-letter word OUR could be used to form the word FOURSOME, the sentence would not make sense.

12. The completed word in the sentence should read as follows: Celia **CLASPED** her mother's hand tightly. The following three-letter words could be used to complete CL___ED: ODD (CODDLED); RAD (CRADLED); RAW (CRAWLED); AIM (CLAIMED); AMP (CLAMPED); ASH (CLASHED); ASS (CLASSED); EAR (CLEARED); INK (CLINKED); OAK (CLOAKED); OWN (CLOWNED); ARE (CLEARED); and AVE (CLEAVED), however, none of these words complete the sentence correctly.

13. The completed word in the sentence should read as follows: All the students **PANICKED** the day the results came out.

14. The completed word in the sentence should read as follows: The brave shepherd offered himself up as a **SACRIFICE**.

15. The completed word in the sentence should read as follows: The **ELEVATOR** has broken down again.

16. **Breakfast** and **lunch** are the odd ones out because they **are meals**, whereas morning, twilight, and night are times.

17. **Of** and **to** are the odd ones out because they **are prepositions**, whereas the, an, and a are determiners.

18. **Speed** and **race** are the odd ones out because they **are nouns as well as verbs**, whereas fast, quick, and rapid are adjectives.

19. **Ash** and **elm** are the odd ones out because they **are trees**, whereas snapdragon, daffodil, and peony are flowers.

20. **Confute** and **collage** are the odd ones out because **confute is a verb meaning to prove someone, or something, wrong** and a **collage is a type of picture made by gluing pieces of materials (e.g. photographs, cloth, etc.) to a surface**, whereas conform, obey, and comply are synonymous verbs meaning to be obedient to someone or something (often laws, rules, social conventions etc.).

21. The only two words that form a proper word when combined are **some** and **thing** to give **something**. Sumthin (sum + thin); sumthing (sum + thing); sumthink (sum + think); somethin (some + thin); and somethink (some + think) are all incorrect spellings of the word 'something'.

22. The only two words that form a proper word when combined are **bell** and **owed** to give **bellowed**. Bellowes (bell + owes) is an incorrect spelling of 'bellows'.

23. The only two words that form a proper word when combined are **par** and **don** to give **pardon**. Parsun (par + sun) is an incorrect spelling of 'parson'; parden (par + den) is an incorrect spelling of 'pardon'; persun (per + sun) is an incorrect spelling of 'person'.

24. The only two words that form a proper word when combined are **sick** and **bed** to give **sickbed**. Poorlea (poor + lea) is an incorrect spelling of 'poorly'; sicklea (sick + lea) is an incorrect spelling of 'sickly'.

25. The only two words that form a proper word when combined are **for** and **age** to give **forage**. Forrage (for + rage) and fourage (four + age) are incorrect spellings of 'forage'.

26. To find the missing letter pair, **O is mirrored to obtain L** and **D is mirrored to obtain W** ⇨ **LW**.

27. To find the missing letter pair, **K moves – 7 places to D** and **P moves – 7 places to I** ⇨ **DI**.

28. To find the missing letter pair, **QJ is a mirror pair (Q is the mirror of J); Q moves – 5 places to L**; and **L is mirrored to obtain O** ⇨ **LO**.

29. To find the missing letter pair, **Y moves – 3 places to V** and **B moves + 2 places to D** ⇨ **VD**.

30. To find the missing letter pair, **B moves – 3 places to Y** and **X moves + 2 places to Z** ⇨ **YZ**.

31. Each time, the first and third numbers are added together; then 2 is added to their sum to get the second number:
5 (16) 9 ⇨ 5 + 9 = 14; 14 + 2 = 16 ● 4 (15) 9 ⇨ 4 + 9 = 13; 13 + 2 = 15 ● 3 (?) 8 ⇨ 3 + 8 = 11; 11 + 2 = **13**

32. Each time, the first and third numbers are multiplied by each other; then 4 is added to their product to get the second number:
4 (12) 2 ⇨ 4 x 2 = 8; 8 + 4 = 12 ● 3 (19) 5 ⇨ 3 x 5 = 15; 15 + 4 = 19 ● **2 (?) 6** ⇨ **2 x 6 = 12; 12 + 4 = 16**

33. Each time, the third number is subtracted from the first number; then 5 is added to the result to get the second number:
12 (14) 3 ⇨ 12 – 3 = 9; 9 + 5 = 14 ● 7 (10) 2 ⇨ 7 – 2 = 5; 5 + 5 = 10 ● **8 (?) 2** ⇨ **8 – 2 = 6; 6 + 5 = 11**

34. Each time, the first and third numbers are multiplied by each other; then 4 is subtracted from their product to get the second number:
2 (16) 10 ⇨ 2 x 10 = 20; 20 – 4 = 16 ● 3 (23) 9 ⇨ 3 x 9 = 27; 27 – 4 = 23 ● **7 (?) 8** ⇨ **7 x 8 = 56; 56 – 4 = 52**

35. Each time, the third number is subtracted from the first number; then the result is divided by 2 to get the second number:
20 (3) 14 ⇨ 20 – 14 = 6; 6 ÷ 2 = 3 ● 11 (1) 9 ⇨ 11 – 9 = 2; 2 ÷ 2 = 1 ● **15 (?) 7** ⇨ **15 – 7 = 8; 8 ÷ 2 = 4**

36. A comparison of the given three numbers and four words reveals that only two of the given numbers end in 4 and that only two words end with D, so **D = 4**. Therefore:
   - The code for RAID must be either 7524 or 2694
   - The code for WORD must be either 7524 or 2694

Comparing the letters for RAID and WORD with their only two possible codes shows that the words have only one more letter in common: R, and, that the two possible codes have only one more number in common: 2, so **R = 2**. Therefore:
   - The code for **RAID must be 2694**
   - The code for **WORD must be 7524**

Therefore: **R = 2; D = 4; A = 6; W = 7; I = 9**; and **O = 5**. Using these, we can deduce that the code for **DRAW is 4267**. So, **by elimination, the code for DRAM has to be 4261**.

37. As we know that the code for DRAW is 4267, **by substitution**, we can work out that **the code for WARD is 7624**.

38. As we know that 6 = A; 9 = I; 4 = D; 1 = M, **by substitution**, we can work out that **1694 stands for MAID**.

39. A comparison of the given three numbers and four words reveals that while two words begin with the same letter: L, none of the numbers start with the same digit. Therefore, the code for either LINE or LONE is missing. However, two of the words have the same second letter: I (i.e. HILT and LINE) while two of the numbers have the same second digit 4 (i.e. 2463 and 6475). Therefore:
   - The code for HILT must be either 2463 or 6475
   - The code for LINE must be either 2463 or 6475

So the missing code belongs to LONE. Consequently, **by elimination, the code for ONLY must be 8769**.

40. As we know that the code for ONLY is 8769, this means that: **O = 8; N = 7; L = 6; Y = 9**. Using these, we can deduce that the code for **HILT is 2463** and that the code for **LINE is 6475**. Therefore: **H = 2; I = 4; T = 3; E = 5**. From all this, **by substitution**, we can work out that **the code 8469 stands for OILY**.

41. As we know all the codes for all the letters, **by substitution**, we can deduce that **the code 3846 stands for TOIL**.

42. Using the given information, we can deduce the following:
   - A. Gemma has five aunts ⇨ might be true. Although we know that Gemma's mother has two sisters, we do not know whether Gemma's father has any sisters, nor do we know whether her father's brothers are

29

married or not.

- B. Gemma's parents have four children ⇨ is true. They have Gemma, Gemma's brother, and Gemma's two sisters.
- C. Gemma only has four cousins ⇨ **cannot be true. Gemma has at least five cousins. Her uncle (her father's brother) has at least one child, and, between them, her aunts have four children (each aunt has two children).**
- D. Gemma's father has no sisters ⇨ might be true. We do not know if Gemma's father has any sisters.
- E. Gemma is eleven years old ⇨ might be true. We are not told how old Gemma is.

43. In the first two pairs, the following pattern is used to make the second word of each pair:

i n d i **g o** ⇨ **go**   n e a r **b y** ⇨ **by**
        1 2   1 2

The result of applying this pattern to the first word of the third pair is as follows:

f r **u** i **t**
      1 2

The letters to be used, therefore, are **i, t** and they are to be kept in this order – i.e. **it**.

44. In the first two pairs, the following pattern is used to make the second word of each pair:

r e l **a** t **e** ⇨ real   **d** i **l a** t **e** ⇨ dial
1 2 4 3   1 24 3

The result of applying this pattern to the first word of the third pair is as follows:

m e l a n g e
1 243

The letters to be used, therefore, are **m, e, l, a** and need to be re-ordered as **m, e, a, l = meal**.

45. In the first two pairs, the following pattern is used to make the second word of each pair:

c a l f ⇨ lac<u>e</u>   r a c k ⇨ car<u>e</u>
3 21   3 21

The result of applying this pattern to the first word of the third pair is as follows:

d a f t
3 21

The letters to be used, therefore, are **d, a, f** and they are to be re-ordered as **f, a, d**. Additionally, a fourth letter 'e' should be added at the end. This makes the missing word of the third pair **fade**.

46. In the first two pairs, the following pattern is used to make the second word of each pair:

a **t** t **i r e** ⇨ tire   e **n** t **i c e** ⇨ nice
1 234   1 234

The result of applying this pattern to the first word of the third pair is as follows:

i **m** p **a l e**
1 234

The letters to be used, therefore, are **m, a, l, e** and they are to be kept in this order – i.e. **male**.

47. In the first two pairs, the following pattern is used to make the second word of each pair:

l **i** t t **l**e ⇨ it   c **a** t t l **e** ⇨ at
12   12

The result of applying this pattern to the first word of the third pair is as follows:

s **t** o **r** m y
12

The letters to be used, therefore, are **t, o** and they are to be kept in this order – i.e. **to**.

48. The one word from the list that relates to both groups of words is **appeal**.
- *Appeal (n.) is* a request (often formal) for help, money, action, etc. *(i.e. 'request'; 'plea' - 1st group).*
- *Appeal (n.) is* the state, or condition, of being attractive, pleasing, interesting, etc. *(i.e. 'attraction'; 'interest' - 2nd group).*

49. The one word from the list that relates to both groups of words is **stall**.
- *Stall (n.) is* a temporary stand set up in a market or at a fair *(i.e. 'stand'; 'kiosk' - 1st group).*

- **Stall (v.)** *is to do something in order to delay (I.e. 'delay'; 'postpone' - 2nd group).*

50. The one word from the list that relates to both groups of words is **tend**.
    - **Tend (v.)** *is to take care of someone or something (i.e. 'nurse'; 'nurture' - 1st group).*
    - **Tend (v.)** *is to slope or to lean in a particular direction (i.e. 'lean'; 'incline' - 2nd group).*

51. The one word from the list that relates to both groups of words is **cane**.
    - **Cane (n.)** *is 1. a walking stick 2. a stick used for beating someone as a type of punishment (i.e. 'staff'; 'rod' - 1st group).*
    - **Cane (v.)** *is to hit someone with a cane as punishment (i.e. 'beat'; 'hit' - 2nd group).*

52. The one word from the list that relates to both groups of words is **hasty**.
    - **Hasty (adj.)** *is being impulsive; acting or speaking without thinking; not preparing before doing something (i.e. 'reckless'; 'impulsive' - 1st group).*
    - **Hasty (adj.)** *is being swift or quick (i.e. 'rapid'; 'speedy' - 2nd group).*

53. The analogy common to both pairs is that of **antonyms**. **Here** is the antonym of <u>there</u>, and **this** is the antonym of <u>that</u>.

54. The analogy common to both pairs is that of **countries and their capital cities**. <u>Rome</u> is the capital city of **Italy**; <u>Berlin</u> is the capital city of **Germany**.

55. The analogy common to both pairs is that of **homophones** (i.e. words that sound the same, but which are spelt differently and have different meanings). **Current** and <u>currant</u> are homophones; **feet** and <u>feat</u> are homophones.

56. The analogy common to both pairs is that of **birds and their colours**. A **canary** is a bird that is <u>yellow</u> in colour; a **crow** is a bird that is <u>black</u> in colour.

57. The analogy common to both pairs is that of **idioms** (i.e. common sayings that frequently do not mean what their individual words suggest). We say that something is as **flat** as a <u>pancake</u>; similarly, we say that something is as **light** as a <u>feather</u>.

58. The analogy common to both pairs is that of **collective nouns**. **Litter** is the collective noun for <u>puppies</u>; **pack** is the collective noun for <u>wolves</u>.

59. The analogy common to both pairs is that of **antonyms**. **Hit** is the antonym of <u>miss</u>; **stop** is the antonym of <u>go</u>.

60. To see the numerical problem, we substitute the letters for their given values:

    $$C \div A \times B \div E \quad \Rightarrow \quad 16 \div 8 \times 12 \div 6$$

    By carrying out the mathematical operations in stages, we arrive at the numerical answer of the problem:

    $$16 \div 8 = 2 \quad 2 \times 12 = 24 \quad 24 \div 6 = \mathbf{4}$$

    As the number 4 is represented by the letter D, the answer is **D**.

61. To see the numerical problem, we substitute the letters for their given values:

    $$3B \div C \quad \Rightarrow \quad 3 \times 4 \div 6$$

    By carrying out the mathematical operations in stages, we arrive at the numerical answer of the problem:

    $$3 \times 4 = 12 \quad 12 \div 6 = \mathbf{2}$$

    As the number 2 is represented by the letter A, the answer is **A**.

62. To see the numerical problem, we substitute the letters for their given values:

    $$B(A + C) \div D \quad \Rightarrow \quad 3 \times (1 + 5) \div 6$$

    By carrying out the mathematical operations in stages, we arrive at the numerical answer of the problem:

    $$3 \times (1 + 5) = 3 \times 6 \quad 3 \times 6 = 18 \quad 18 \div 6 = \mathbf{3}$$

    As the number 3 is represented by the letter B, the answer is **B**.

63. To see the numerical problem, we substitute the letters for their given values:

    $$E - C \div B + A \quad \Rightarrow \quad 18 - 6 \div 4 + 3$$

    By carrying out the mathematical operations in stages, we arrive at the numerical answer of the problem:

    $$18 - 6 = 12 \quad 12 \div 4 = 3 \quad 3 + 3 = \mathbf{6}$$

    As the number 6 is represented by the letter C, the answer is **C**.

64. To see the numerical problem, we substitute the letters for their given values:

    $$(C + D + E) - 2E \quad \Rightarrow \quad (5 + 6 + 9) - (2 \times 9)$$

    By carrying out the mathematical operations in stages, we arrive at the numerical answer of the problem:

    $$(5 + 6 + 9) = 20 \quad 20 - (2 \times 9) = 20 - 18 \quad 20 - 18 = \mathbf{2}$$

    As the number 2 is represented by the letter A, the answer is **A**.

65. This is a **complex code** which is obtained by moving the letters of the word using the sequence **+ 1, + 2, + 3, + 4, + 5**. Hence, the code for CANDY is found in the following way: **C + 1 place = D; A + 2 places = C; N + 3 places = Q; D + 4 places = H; Y + 5 places = D**. The code for **CANDY** is, therefore, **DCQHD**.

66. This is a **complex code** which is obtained by moving each letter of the word **+ 2 places**. Hence, the code for AVENUE is found in the following way: **A + 2 places = C; V + 2 places = X; E + 2 places = G; N + 2 places = P; U + 2 places = W; E + 2 places = G**. The code for **AVENUE** is, therefore, **CXGPWG**.

67. This is a **mirror code** where each letter and its code are equal distances from the middle of the alphabet (i.e. the space between M and N). Hence, the code for FAIN is found in the following way: **the mirror reflection of F = U; the mirror reflection of A = Z; the mirror reflection of I = R; the mirror reflection of N = M**. The code for **FAIN** is, therefore, **UZRM**.

68. This is a **simple code** where each letter and its code are as follows: S is encoded as F; H is encoded as Q; O is encoded as P; R is encoded as N; E is encoded as C. Hence, the word that the code QPNFC stands for is found in the following way: **Q is the code for H; P is the code for O; N is the code for R; F is the code for S; C is the code for E**. The word that the code **QPNFC** stands for is, therefore, **HORSE**.

69. This is a **mirror code** where each letter and its code are equal distances from the middle of the alphabet (i.e. the space between M and N). Hence, the code for STATION is found in the following way: **the mirror reflection of S = H; the mirror reflection of T = G; the mirror reflection of A = Z; the mirror reflection of T = G; the mirror reflection of I = R; the mirror reflection of O = L; the mirror reflection of N = M**. The code for **STATION** is, therefore, **HGZGRLM**.

70. Using the information given, we can deduce that each child bought the following types of books, and, that of all the children, __Anne bought the fewest books__:

Anne	Sarah	Ahmed	Ali	Michel
~~Sci-fi~~	Sci-fi	Sci-fi	Sci-fi	Sci-fi
Dinosaurs	Dinosaurs			Dinosaurs
~~Wimpy~~	Wimpy	Wimpy	Wimpy	Wimpy
		Aeroplanes		

71. This number sequence is formed by **adding 3 to each number to obtain the next term**:

$$1 (+ 3 =) 4 (+ 3 =) 7 (+ 3 =) 10 (+ 3 =) 13$$

According to this pattern, the next term in this sequence is 13 (+ 3 =) **16**.

72. This number sequence is formed of **two alternating series**. In the first series: 4, 7, 5, 6, 6, the next term is obtained by **adding 1**:

$$4 (+ 1 =) 5 (+ 1 =) 6$$

In the second series: 4, 7, 5, 6, 6, the next term is obtained by **subtracting 1**:

$$7 (- 1 =) 6$$

As the next term in the sequence belongs to the second series, the term will be 6 (- 1 =) **5**.

73. This number sequence is formed by **adding every two consecutive terms together to obtain the next one**:

$$1 (+) 2 (=) 3 (+ 2 =) 5 (+ 3 =) 8$$

According to this pattern, the next term in this sequence is **8 (+ 5 =) 13**.

74. This number sequence is formed of **two alternating series**. In the first series: 7, 3, 6, 5, 5, the next term is obtained by **subtracting 1**:

$$7 (- 1 =) 6 (- 1 =) 5$$

In the second series: 7, 3, 6, 5, 5, the next term is obtained by **adding 2**:

$$3 (+ 2 =) 5$$

As the next term in the sequence belongs to the second series, the term will be **5 (+ 2 =) 7**.

75. This number sequence is formed by **subtracting descending odd numbers from each term to obtain the next, beginning with the odd number 11**:

$$36 (- 11 =) 25 (- 9 =) 16 (- 7 =) 9$$

According to this pattern, the next term in this sequence is 9 (- 5 =) **4**.

76. The first set of words is governed by the following rule:

n a m e (m a t) t i l l
2 1   1 2 3 3

By applying this rule to the second set of words we can see the following:

h <u>o</u> l e (?) g a m e
  2 1   3

The letters to be used, therefore, are **o, l, g** and need to be re-ordered as: **l, o, g = <u>log</u>**.

77. The first set of words is governed by the following rule:

<u>o</u> m e n (**m o d e**) i <u>d</u> l <u>e</u>
2 1   1 2 3 4   3 4

By applying this rule to the second set of words we can see the following:

<u>m</u> e n d (?) l i <u>s</u> <u>t</u>
2 1   3 4

The letters to be used, therefore, are **m, e, i, t** and need to be re-ordered as: **e, m, i, t = <u>emit</u>**.

78. The first set of words is governed by the following rule:

b a <u>n</u> <u>g</u> (**r i n g**) <u>i</u> <u>r</u> a t e
   3 4 1 2 3 4 2 1

By applying this rule to the second set of words we can see the following:

p a <u>r</u> <u>t</u> (?) <u>o</u> <u>f</u> f e r
   3 4   2 1

The letters to be used, therefore, are **r, t, o, f** and need to be re-ordered as: **f, o, r, t = <u>fort</u>**.

79. The first set of words is governed by the following rule:

l <u>a</u> <u>m</u> <u>e</u> (**m e a t**) o u <u>t</u> i n g
  3 1 2 1 2 3 4   4

By applying this rule to the second set of words we can see the following:

w <u>a</u> <u>v</u> <u>e</u> (?) a l <u>l</u> o w s
  3 1 2   4

The letters to be used, therefore, are **a, v, e, l** and need to be re-ordered as: **v, e, a, l = <u>veal</u>**.

80. The first set of words is governed by the following rule:

b <u>o</u> <u>o</u> k (**t o o l**) <u>t</u> e l <u>l</u>
  2 3 1 2 3 4 1 4

By applying this rule to the second set of words we can see the following:

m <u>a</u> <u>z</u> e (?) <u>l</u> a c <u>y</u>
  2 3   1 4

The letters to be used, therefore, are **a, z, l, y** and need to be re-ordered as: **l, a, z, y = <u>lazy</u>**.

1. To see the numerical problem, we substitute the letters for their given values:

$$C \div A \times D \div B \quad \Rightarrow \quad 6 \div 3 \times 12 \div 4$$

By carrying out the mathematical operations in stages, we arrive at the numerical answer of the problem:

$$6 \div 3 = 2 \quad 2 \times 12 = 24 \quad 24 \div 4 = 6$$

As the number 6 is represented by the letter C, the answer is **C**.

2. To see the numerical problem, we substitute the letters for their given values:

$$3C - (D + B) \quad \Rightarrow \quad 3 \times 5 - (7 + 4)$$

By carrying out the mathematical operations in stages, we arrive at the numerical answer of the problem:

$$3 \times 5 = 15 \quad 15 - (7 + 4) = 15 - 11 \quad 15 - 11 = 4$$

As the number 4 is represented by the letter B, the answer is **B**.

3. To see the numerical problem, we substitute the letters for their given values:

$$E \times D \div B \div A \quad \Rightarrow \quad 12 \times 6 \div 4 \div 3$$

By carrying out the mathematical operations in stages, we arrive at the numerical answer of the problem:

$$12 \times 6 = 72 \quad 72 \div 4 = 18 \quad 18 \div 3 = 6$$

As the number 6 is represented by the letter D, the answer is **D**.

4. To see the numerical problem, we substitute the letters for their given values:

$$2A \times D - BC \quad \Rightarrow \quad (2 \times 1) \times 8 - (3 \times 5)$$

By carrying out the mathematical operations in stages, we arrive at the numerical answer of the problem:

$$(2 \times 1) = 2 \quad 2 \times 8 = 16 \quad 16 - (3 \times 5) = 16 - 15 \quad 16 - 15 = 1$$

As the number 1 is represented by the letter A, the answer is **A**.

5. To see the numerical problem, we substitute the letters for their given values:

$$(B^2 - D) + 3A \div C \quad \Rightarrow \quad (5^2 - 7) + (3 \times 4) \div 6$$

By carrying out the mathematical operations in stages, we arrive at the numerical answer of the problem:

$$(5^2 - 7) = (25 - 7) \quad (25 - 7) = 18 \quad 18 + (3 \times 4) = 18 + 12 \quad 18 + 12 = 30 \quad 30 \div 6 = 5$$

As the number 5 is represented by the letter B, the answer is **B**.

6. In the first two pairs, the following pattern is used to make the second word of each pair:

t o t t e r s ⇨ **tort**
1 2   4   3

s e a t i n g ⇨ **sent**
1 2   4   3

The result of applying this pattern to the first word of the third pair is as follows:

c o n d o l e
1 2   4   3

The letters to be used, therefore, are **c, o, d, l** and need to be re-ordered as: **c, o, l, d = cold**.

7. In the first two pairs, the following pattern is used to make the second word of each pair:

h a t e r ⇨ ha_l_ter
1 2 3 4 5

t a k e r ⇨ ta_l_ker
1 2 3 4 5

The result of applying this pattern to the first word of the third pair is as follows:

s a v e d
1 2 3 4 5

The letters that are to be used, therefore, are **s, a, v, e, d** and are to be kept in this order. Additionally, the letter 'l' is to be inserted after the second letter of the word (i.e. 'a'). This makes the missing word of the third pair: **s, a, l, v, e, d = salved**.

8. In the first two pairs, the following pattern is used to make the second word of each pair:

m o n s o o n ⇨ **moon**
1   2 3 4

p h a r m a c y ⇨ **pacy**
1   2 3 4

The result of applying this pattern to the first word of the third pair is as follows:

d e l i b e r a t e
1   2 3 4

The letters to be used, therefore, are **d, a, t, e** and are to be kept in this order – i.e. **date**.

9. In the first two pairs, the following pattern is used to make the second word of each pair:

s p i n n e r ⇨ nip   s t a p l e ⇨ pat
   3 2 1   3 2 1

The result of applying this pattern to the first word of the third pair is as follows:

s w o l l e n
   3 2 1

The letters to be used, therefore, are **w, o, l** and need to be re-ordered as: **l, o, w = low**.

10. In the first two pairs, the following pattern is used to make the second word of each pair:

p o t t e r ⇨ poet   s l i d e r ⇨ sled
1 2   4 3   1 2   4 3

The result of applying this pattern to the first word of the third pair is as follows:

p o m m e l
1 2   4 3

The letters to be used, therefore, are **p, o, m, e** and need to be re-ordered as: **p, o, e, m = poem**.

11. The one word from the list that relates to both groups of words is **dart**.
    - *Dart (n.)* is a weapon that is narrow and pointed (often small) which can be fired or thrown *(i.e. 'arrow'; 'bolt' - 1st group)*.
    - *Dart (v.)* is to move quickly and suddenly *(i.e. 'dash'; 'flit' - 2nd group)*.

12. The one word from the list that relates to both groups of words is **rich**.
    - *Rich (adj.)* is possessing or having a great deal of money *(i.e. 'wealthy'; 'affluent' - 1st group)*.
    - *Rich (adj.)* is 1. being food containing a lot of fat, oil, butter, dried fruit, etc. 2. being food that is strongly seasoned or having a strong taste *(i.e. 'creamy'; 'tasty' - 2nd group)*.

13. The one word from the list that relates to both groups of words is **trip**.
    - *Trip (n.)* is a short or brief journey to a place *(i.e. 'journey'; 'tour' - 1st group)*.
    - *Trip (v.)* is to misplace one's foot (or feet) when walking, which might result in falling over *(i.e. 'stumble'; 'tumble' - 2nd group)*.

14. The one word from the list that relates to both groups of words is **rise**.
    - *Rise (v.)* is to move upwards or in an upwards direction *(i.e. 'ascend'; 'escalate' - 1st group)*.
    - *Rise (v.)* is to fight against, or to openly resist, an authority; to rebel *(i.e. 'rebel'; 'revolt' - 2nd group)*.

15. The one word from the list that relates to both groups of words is **periodically**.
    - *Periodically (adv.)* is in a way that takes place from time to time *(i.e. 'occasionally'; 'sporadically' - 1st group)*.
    - *Periodically (adv.)* is in a way that occurs at regular intervals *(i.e. 'regularly'; 'cyclically' - 2nd group)*.

16. To find the missing letter pair, **L moves – 4 places to H and N moves + 6 places to T ⇨ HT**.

17. To find the missing letter pair, **WD is a mirror pair (W is the mirror of D); W moves – 5 places to R; R is then mirrored to obtain I ⇨ RI**.

18. To find the missing letter pair, **B moves + 4 places to F and M moves – 6 places to G ⇨ FG**.

19. To find the missing letter pair, **G is mirrored to obtain T; I is mirrored to obtain R; the resultant mirror pair TR is then inverted to obtain RT ⇨ RT**.

20. To find the missing letter pair, **JQ is a mirror pair (J is the mirror of Q); J moves + 4 places to N; N is then mirrored to obtain M ⇨ NM**.

21. The hidden **four-letter word** is **vale**: Jim stared as the floating o**val e**longated.

22. The hidden **four-letter word** is **heal**: T**he al**ligator's vicious jaws opened wide.

23. The hidden **four-letter word** is **deli**: The Ancient Egyptians ma**de li**nen garments.

24. The hidden **four-letter word** is **call**: Albion is a wonderful, mysti**cal l**and.

25. The hidden **four-letter word** is **area**: Local councils **are a**bolishing parking fines.

26. Using the given information, we can deduce that the children who finished the race – along with their speeds and positions – are as follows:

Oscar	Ella	Lamia	Arthur
37 seconds	36 seconds	33 seconds	32 seconds
(33 + 4)	(33 + 3)		(37 − 5)
4th	3rd	2nd	1st

Therefore:

- A. Arthur completed the race in 34 seconds ⇨ is not true as he finished in 32 seconds.
- B. Lamia finished in second place ⇨ **is true**.
- C. Oscar came third ⇨ is not true as he came in fourth place.
- D. Fiona tripped over ⇨ might be true. We are told that she 'dropped her egg just before the finishing line', but we are not told why she did so.
- E. Ella was disqualified ⇨ is not true as we are told she finished the race.

27. Each time, the first and third numbers are added together; then their sum is multiplied by 3 to get the second number:
21 (72) 3 ⇨ 21 + 3 = 24; 24 x 3 = 72 ● 9 (30) 1 ⇨ 9 + 1 = 10; 10 x 3 = 30 ● **22 (?) 3 ⇨ 22 + 3 = 25; 25 x 3 = <u>75</u>**

28. Each time, the third number is subtracted from the first number; then the result of the subtraction is divided by 7 to get the second number:
70 (4) 42 ⇨ 70 − 42 = 28; 28 ÷ 7 = 4 ● 49 (4) 21 ⇨ 49 − 21 = 28; 28 ÷ 7 = 4 ● 63 (?) 14 ⇨ 63 − 14 = 49; 49 ÷ 7 = <u>7</u>

29. Each time, the square roots of the first and third numbers are found; the results are added together; then 5 is added to their sum to get the second number:
36 (14) 9 ⇨ √36 = 6; √9 = 3; 6 + 3 = 9; 9 + 5 = 14 ● 25 (12) 4 ⇨ √25 = 5; √4 = 2; 5 + 2 = 7; 7 + 5 = 12 ●
64 (?) 49 ⇨ √64 = 8; √49 = 7; 8 + 7 = 15; 15 + 5 = <u>20</u>

30. Each time, the first and third numbers are added together; then 8 is subtracted from their sum to get the second number:
39 (36) 5 ⇨ 39 + 5 = 44; 44 − 8 = 36 ● 67 (80) 21 ⇨ 67 + 21 = 88; 88 − 8 = 80 ● 52 (?) 16 ⇨ 52 + 16 = 68; 68 − 8 = <u>60</u>

31. Each time, the third number is subtracted from the first number; then the result of the subtraction is multiplied by 8 to get the second number:
5 (32) 1 ⇨ 5 − 1 = 4; 4 x 8 = 32 ● 4 (16) 2 ⇨ 4 − 2 = 2; 2 x 8 = 16 ● **7 (?) 2 ⇨ 7 − 2 = 5; 5 x 8 = <u>40</u>**

32. By removing <u>**O**</u> from <u>O</u>WED and adding it to ROT, we get the new words: **WED   ROOT**. While D can be removed from OWED to give OWE, the D cannot be added to ROT in any way to form a proper word. Similarly, while E can be added to ROT to give ROTE, OWD is not a proper word.

33. By removing <u>**P**</u> from CLAMP and adding it to HOPED, we get the new words: **CLAM   HOPPED**. While C can be removed from CLAMP to give LAMP; M can be removed from CLAMP to give CLAP; and L can be removed from CLAMP to give CAMP, none of these three letters (i.e. C, M, L) can be added to HOPED to form a proper word.

34. By removing <u>**R**</u> from WO<u>R</u>E and adding it to ANGER, we get the new words: **WOE   RANGER**. While W can be removed from WORE to give ORE, W cannot be added to ANGER in any way to form a proper word.

35. By removing <u>**F**</u> from <u>F</u>RANK and adding it to SOT, we get the new words: **RANK   SOFT**. While R in FRANK can be added to SOT to give SORT, and N can be added to SOT to give SNOT, neither FANK nor FRAK is a proper word.

36. By removing <u>**the first E**</u> from <u>E</u>MERGE and adding it to LAD, we get the new words: **MERGE   LEAD**. While the second and third Es can be removed from EMERGE and added to LAD to give LEAD, neither EMRGE nor EMERG is a proper word.

37. Each term in this letter sequence consists of two capital letters. The first capital letter in each term **moves according to the pattern + 4, − 1, + 4, − 1**:
$$J (+ 4 =) N (− 1 =) M (+ 4 =) Q (− 1 =) P$$
Hence, the first capital letter of the next term of the sequence is **P (+ 4 =) <u>T</u>**. The second capital letter in each term **moves according to the pattern + 1, − 5, + 1, − 5**:
$$J (+ 1 =) K (− 5 =) F (+ 1 =) G (− 5 =) B$$
Hence, the second capital letter of the next term of the sequence is **B (+ 1 =) <u>C</u>**. Thus, the next complete term of this sequence is <u>TC</u>.

38. Each term in this letter sequence consists of three capital letters. The first capital letter in each term **moves + 2 places every time**:
$$N (+ 2 =) P (+ 2 =) R (+ 2 =) T$$
Hence, the first capital letter of the next term of the sequence is **T (+ 2 =) <u>V</u>**. The second capital letter in each term **moves + 4 places every time**:

$$D (+ 4 =) H (+ 4 -) L (+ 4 =) P$$

Hence, the second capital letter of the next term of the sequence is **P (+ 4 =)** T. The third capital letter in each term **moves – 6 places every time**:

$$X (- 6 =) R (- 6 =) L (- 6 =) F$$

Hence, the third capital letter of the next term of the sequence is **F (– 6 =)** Z. Thus, the next complete term of this sequence is **VTZ**.

39. This letter sequence is formed of two alternating series of capital letters. Each term of each series consists of a single capital letter. In the first series of the sequence: C, I, I, K, N, M, R, the capital letters **move according to the pattern + 6, + 5, + 4**:

$$C (+ 6 =) I (+ 5 =) N (+ 4 =) R$$

In the second series of the sequence: C, I, I, K, N, M, R, the capital letters **move + 2 places every time**:

$$I (+ 2 =) K (+ 2 =) M$$

As the next term of the sequence belongs to the second series, the next term will be **M (+ 2 =)** O. Thus, the next complete term of this sequence is **O**.

40. Each term in this sequence is formed of a number and a capital letter. The number in each term **moves – 4 places every time**:

$$25 (- 4 =) 21 (- 4 =) 17 (- 4 =) 13$$

Hence, the number of the next term of the sequence is **13 (– 4 =)** 9. The capital letter in each term **moves + 3 places every time**:

$$C (+ 3 =) F (+ 3 =) I (+ 3 =) L$$

Hence, the capital letter of the next term of the sequence is **L (+ 3 =)** O. Thus, the next complete term of this sequence is **9O**.

41. Each term in this sequence is formed of a number, a capital letter, and a lower-case letter. The number in each term **moves according to the pattern – 2, – 3, – 2**:

$$12 (- 2 =) 10 (- 3 =) 7 (- 2 =) 5$$

Hence, the number of the next term of the sequence is **5 (– 3 =)** 2. The capital letter in each term **moves according to the pattern + 3, – 2, + 3**:

$$T (+ 3 =) W (- 2 =) U (+ 3 =) X$$

Hence, the capital letter of the next term of the sequence is **X (– 2 =)** V. The lower-case letter in each term **moves according to the pattern + 3, + 1, + 3**:

$$t (+ 3 =) w (+ 1 =) x (+ 3 =) a$$

Hence, the lower-case letter of the next term of the sequence is **a (+ 1 =)** b. Thus, the next complete term of this sequence is **2Vb**.

42. Each term in this sequence is formed of a capital letter and a number. The capital letter in each term **moves according to the pattern + 2, – 1, + 2**:

$$D (+ 2 =) F (- 1 =) E (+ 2 =) G$$

Hence, the capital letter of the next term of the sequence is **G (– 1 =)** F. The number in each term **moves according to the pattern – 1, – 2, – 3**:

$$19 (- 1 =) 18 (- 2 =) 16 (- 3 =) 13$$

Hence, the number of the next term of the sequence is **13 (– 4 =)** 9. Thus, the next complete term of this sequence is **F9**.

43. Each term in this sequence is formed of a single capital letter. Each time, the capital letter **moves according to the pattern – 6, – 4, – 2, – 0**:

$$G (- 6 =) A (- 4 =) W (- 2 =) U (- 0 =) U$$

Hence, the capital letter of the next term of the sequence is **U (+ 2 =)** W. Thus, the next complete term of this sequence is **W**.

44. The two words closest in meaning in the two given sets are **nail (n.)** and **tack (n.)**.
   - *Nail (n.)* is an object that resembles a spike which is hammered into something and which is made of metal.
   - *Tack (n.)* is a type of nail.

45. The two words closest in meaning in the two given sets are **choose (v.)** and **select (v.)**.
   - *Choose (v.)* is to make a selection of something or several things from amongst a larger group.
   - *Select (v.)* is to choose something or several things from amongst a larger group.

46. The two words closest in meaning in the two given sets are **evenly (adv.)** and **coolly (adv.)**.

- *Evenly (adv.) is* in a calm way or manner.
- *Coolly (adv.) is* in a calm way or manner.

47. The two words closest in meaning in the two given sets are <u>keepsake (n.)</u> and <u>memento (n.)</u>.
- ***Keepsake (n.) is*** an item that is kept (and often treasured) as a reminder of a person, place, etc.
- ***Memento (n.) is*** an item that is kept (and often treasured) as a reminder of a person, place, etc.

48. The two words closest in meaning in the two given sets are <u>beside (prep.)</u> and <u>adjacent (prep.)</u>.
- ***Beside (prep.) is*** being next to, near, or by the side of someone or something.
- ***Adjacent (prep.) is*** being next to, or lying next to, someone or something.

49. The first set of words is governed by the following rule:

a p p l e s (p a w s) s o w n
2 1   1 2 3 4 4 3

By applying this rule to the second set of words we can see the following:

i n k i e r (?) d o n e
2 1   4 3

The letters to be used, therefore, are **i, k, d, n** and need to be re-ordered as: **k, i, n, d = <u>kind</u>**.

50. The first set of words is governed by the following rule:

s m e l l (m i l e) p i n k
1 4 3   1 2 3 4   2

By applying this rule to the second set of words we can see the following:

s t e m s (?) g a n g
1 4 3   2

The letters to be used, therefore, are **t, e, m, a** and need to be re-ordered as: **t, a, m, e = <u>tame</u>**.

51. The first set of words is governed by the following rule:

d a m e (m a r k) f o r k
2 1   1 2 3 4   3 4

By applying this rule to the second set of words we can see the following:

r i s e (?) b a r e
2 1   3 4

The letters to be used, therefore, are **i, s, r, e** and need to be re-ordered as: **s, i, r, e = <u>sire</u>**.

52. The first set of words is governed by the following rule:

e a s y (y e a r) r a r e
2 3 1 1 2 3 4 4

By applying this rule to the second set of words we can see the following:

a n e w (?) d i r t
2 3 1   4

The letters to be used, therefore, are **a, n, w, d** and need to be re-ordered as: **w, a, n, d = <u>wand</u>**.

53. The first set of words is governed by the following rule:

s u p p e r (p u s h) h a r m
3 2 1   1 2 3 4 4

By applying this rule to the second set of words we can see the following:

l a u g h s (?) e n d s
3 2 1   4

The letters to be used, therefore, are **l, a, g, e** and need to be re-ordered as: **g, a, l, e = <u>gale</u>**.

54. The first set of words is governed by the following rule:

c o a l (c o r e) a r e a
1 2   1 2 3 4   3 4

By applying this rule to the second set of words we can see the following:

j u m p (?) s t e m
1 2   3 4

The letters to be used, therefore, are **j, u, t, e** and are to be kept in this order – i.e. **jute**.

55. The first set of words is governed by the following rule:

t a l k (r a n k) r i n g
  2 4 1 2 3 4 1 3

By applying this rule to the second set of words we can see the following:

b l e d (?) p o o r
 2 4   1 3

The letters to be used, therefore, are **l, d, p, o** and need to be re-ordered as: **p, l, o, d = plod**.

56. Using the information given, we can deduce which juices each child drinks, and, that of all the juices, **fruit cocktail is the least popular** (viz. only two children - Josh and Sheila - drink it):

Orange	Cranberry	Fruit Cocktail	Grapefruit	Blueberry
Josh	Josh	Josh	Josh	
Sheila		Sheila		
George			~~George~~	George
	Neville		Neville	Neville
	Mike		Mike	Mike

57. Using the information given, we can deduce which attractions each tourist visits, and, that of all the tourists, **Gerhardt is the person who visits the most tourist attractions** (viz. 4):

London Eye	Buckingham Palace	Madame Tussaud's	British Museum	National Gallery
Bertrand	Bertrand			
Francois	Francois		Francois	
	Aisha	Aisha		
		Alaa		Alaa
Gerhardt	Gerhardt	Gerhardt		Gerhardt

58. A comparison of the four given words reveals that all four words contain a penultimate N. At the same time, all three of the given numbers contain a penultimate 5. This means that **the code for N must be 5**.

Comparing all the words also reveals that while two words begin with the same letter: S, none of the numbers begin with the same digit. Therefore, the code for either SING or SONG is missing.

The comparison of the words also shows that although DINE and GONE start with different letters, they both end with the same letter: E. At the same time, two of the given numbers end with the same digit: 7. Hence, **7 must be the code for E**. Hence, too:
- The code for DINE is either 8457 or 3957
- The code for GONE is either 8457 or 3957

Therefore:
- 2953 is the code for either SING or SONG

This means that **S = 2** and **G = 3**. Consequently, using these codes, we can deduce that **the code for GONE is 3957**.

59. As we know that 3957 is the code for GONE, this means that **3 = G; 9 = O; 5 = N; 7 = E**. It also means that **8457 is the code for DINE**. From this, **8 = D; 4 = I; 5 = N; 7 = E**. Therefore, **by substitution**, we can work out that **the code for NINE is 5457**.

60. As we know that 2 = S; 9 = O; 5 = N, **by substitution**, we can work out that **2995 is the code for SOON**.

61. As we know that 2 = S; 9 = O; 5 = N; 7 = E, **by substitution**, we can work out that **5927 is the code for NOSE**.

62. A comparison of the four given words reveals that three out of the four words end with the same letter: E, while only one word ends with N.

As two out of the three given numbers end with the same digit: 9, this must mean that **9 = E**. Hence, **6278 must be the code for DARN**. Therefore: **6 = D; 2 = A; 7 = R; 8 = N**. From this, we can further deduce that:
- **7469 is the code for RUDE**
- **3489 must be the code for TUNE** (since the last remaining word - RUNE - begins with an R which we know is 7, but the number code for which is not given)

Consequently, from all this, we now know that: **6 = D; 2 = A; 7 = R; 8 = N; 4 = U; 9 = E; 3 = T**. Therefore, **by substitution,** we can work out that the **code for RUNE is 7489**.

63. As we know all the codes for all the letters, **by substitution**, we can deduce that **the code for NEAR is 8927**.

64. As we know all the codes for all the letters, **by substitution**, we can deduce that **the code 7483 stands for RUNT**.

65. As we know all the codes for all the letters, **by substitution**, we can deduce that **the code 6279 stands for DARE**.

66. The given equation is as follows: $7 \times 7 - 9 \div 4 = 31 - 4 \div 9 + (?)$. First, solve the left-hand side:

$$7 \times 7 - 9 \div 4 \quad = \quad 49 - 9 \div 4 \quad = \quad 40 \div 4 \quad = \quad \mathbf{10}$$

Then, solve the right-hand side as far as possible:

$$31 - 4 \div 9 + (?) \quad = \quad 27 \div 9 + (?) \quad = \quad \mathbf{3 + (?)}$$

Put the two sides of the equation together: **10 = 3 + (?)**. The missing number is, therefore, **7**.

67. The given equation is as follows: $17 - 5 \times 2 \div 8 = 6 \times 8 \div 12 - (?)$. First, solve the left-hand side:

$$17 - 5 \times 2 \div 8 \quad = \quad 12 \times 2 \div 8 \quad = \quad 24 \div 8 \quad = \quad \mathbf{3}$$

Then, solve the right-hand side as far as possible:

$$6 \times 8 \div 12 - (?) \quad = \quad 48 \div 12 - (?) \quad = \quad \mathbf{4 - (?)}$$

Put the two sides of the equation together: **3 = 4 – (?)**. The missing number is, therefore, **1**.

68. The given equation is as follows: $2 + 14 \div 4 + 8 = 18 \times 2 \div 9 + (?)$. First, solve the left-hand side:

$$2 + 14 \div 4 + 8 \quad = \quad 16 \div 4 + 8 \quad = \quad 4 + 8 \quad = \quad \mathbf{12}$$

Then, solve the right-hand side as far as possible:

$$18 \times 2 \div 9 + (?) \quad = \quad 36 \div 9 + (?) \quad = \quad \mathbf{4 + (?)}$$

Put the two sides of the equation together: **12 = 4 + (?)**. The missing number is, therefore, **8**.

69. The given equation is as follows: $81 \div 3 - 4 \times 2 = 34 \div 2 - 2 \times 3 + (?)$. First, solve the left-hand side:

$$81 \div 3 - 4 \times 2 \quad = \quad 27 - 4 \times 2 \quad = \quad 23 \times 2 \quad = \quad \mathbf{46}$$

Then, solve the right-hand side as far as possible:

$$34 \div 2 - 2 \times 3 + (?) \quad = \quad 17 - 2 \times 3 + (?) \quad = \quad 15 \times 3 + (?) \quad = \quad \mathbf{45 + (?)}$$

Put the two sides of the equation together: **46 = 45 + (?)**. The missing number is, therefore, **1**.

70. The given equation is as follows: $21 + 3 - 9 \div 3 = 39 - 14 + 10 \div (?)$. First, solve the left-hand side:

$$21 + 3 - 9 \div 3 \quad = \quad 24 - 9 \div 3 \quad = \quad 15 \div 3 \quad = \quad \mathbf{5}$$

Then, solve the right-hand side as far as possible:

$$39 - 14 + 10 \div (?) \quad = \quad 25 + 10 \div (?) \quad = \quad \mathbf{35 \div (?)}$$

Put the two sides of the equation together: **5 = 35 ÷ (?)**. The missing number is, therefore, **7**.

71. The completed word in the sentence should read as follows: The orange was so rotten that it was full of **MAGGOTS**. Although the three-letter words NET and PIE could be used to complete MAGS to give MAGNETS and MAGPIES, neither of these words would complete the sentence correctly.

72. The completed word in the sentence should read as follows: When his brother took his toy away from him, Luke **BAWLED** loudly.

73. The completed word in the sentence should read as follows: The young girl was wearing a pink **CARDIGAN**.

74. The completed word in the sentence should read as follows: Sam's behaviour was utterly **UNACCEPTABLE**.

75. The completed word in the sentence should read as follows: My grandmother left me an **EXPENSIVE** ring in her will. The following three-letter words could be used to complete EXSIVE: CUR (EXCURSIVE); PAN (EXPANSIVE); TEN (EXTENSIVE). However, none of these words complete the sentence correctly.

76. The two words most opposite in meaning in the two given sets are **loud (adj.)** and **quiet (adj.)**.
   - *Loud (adj.)* is being noisy or making a big sound.
   - *Quiet (adj.)* is making very little sound or no noise at all.

77. The two words most opposite in meaning in the two given sets are **over (prep.)** and **below (prep.)**.
   - *Over (prep.)* is being in a higher place (e.g. number, value, etc.) than something else.
   - *Below (prep.)* is being in a lower place (e.g. rank, number, degree, etc.) than something else.

78. The two words most opposite in meaning in the two given sets are **fact (n.)** and **fiction (n.)**.
   - *Fact (n.)* is something that is known to be true, to have happened, or to have existed.
   - *Fiction (n.)* is something that is known to be untrue; something that is imagined.

79. The two words most opposite in meaning in the two given sets are **coyly (adv.)** and **brazenly (adv.)**.
   - *Coyly (adv.)* is in a shy way.

- *Brazenly (adv.) is* in a bold way.

80. The two words most opposite in meaning in the two given sets are **blind (adj.)** and **sighted (adj.)**.
    - *Blind (adj.) is* being unable to see.
    - *Sighted (adj.) is* being able to see.

1. The one word from the list that relates to both groups of words is **rank**.
   - *Rank (adj.) is to smell both badly and strongly (i.e. 'disgusting'; 'foul' - 1st group).*
   - *Rank (v.) is to arrange things according to distinct levels of something, often according to ability (i.e. 'class'; 'grade' - 2nd group).*

2. The one word from the list that relates to both groups of words is **miss**.
   - *Miss (v.) is to fail to see or notice the absence of something (i.e. 'overlook'; 'neglect' - 1st group).*
   - *Miss (v.) is to feel (often keenly) the lack or absence of someone or something (i.e. 'mourn'; 'lament' - 2nd group).*

3. The one word from the list that relates to both groups of words is **well**.
   - *Well (adj.) is to be in a good state of health (i.e. 'healthy'; 'sound' - 1st group).*
   - *Well (n.) is a natural source of water (i.e. 'spring'; 'fount' - 2nd group).*

4. The one word from the list that relates to both groups of words is **brew**.
   - *Brew (v.) is to make a beverage (i.e. a drink) by leaving a substance such as leaves or grains in a liquid for a period of time (i.e. 'stew'; 'ferment' - 1st group).*
   - *Brew (v.) is to become stronger and threatening (i.e. 'develop'; 'gather' - 2nd group).*

5. The one word from the list that relates to both groups of words is **hit**.
   - *Hit (v.) is to strike something or someone, often forcefully (i.e. 'wallop'; 'cuff' - 1st group).*
   - *Hit (n.) is something that, or someone who, is very popular or successful (i.e. 'success'; 'winner' - 2nd group).*

6. Using the information given, we can deduce that each child plays the following types of instruments, and, that of all the children, **Barbara plays the least number of instruments** *(viz. 1: the guitar)*:

Sally	Barbara	Monica	Sonia	Ola
Violin	~~Violin~~	Violin	Violin	Violin
Flute	~~Flute~~			
Guitar	Guitar	Guitar		Guitar
~~Piano~~	~~Piano~~	Piano	Piano	
		Harp	Harp	

7. This number sequence is formed of **two alternating series**. In the first series: 1, 2, 3, 4, 6, 7, 10, 11, the next term is obtained by **following the pattern + 2, + 3, + 4**:

   $$1 (+ 2 =) 3 (+ 3 =) 6 (+ 4 =) 10$$

   In the second series: 1, 2, 3, 4, 6, 7, 10, 11, the next term is also obtained by **following the pattern + 2, + 3, + 4**:

   $$2 (+ 2 =) 4 (+ 3 =) 7 (+ 4 =) 11$$

   As the next term in the sequence belongs to the first series, the term will be 10 (+ 5 =) **15**.

8. The terms of this number sequence are obtained by **following the pattern – 11, – 9, – 7, – 5**:

   $$73 (- 11 =) 62 (- 9 =) 53 (- 7 =) 46 (- 5 =) 41$$

   According to this pattern, the next term in this sequence is 41 (– 3 =) **38**.

9. This number sequence is formed of **the squares of consecutive numbers in descending order beginning with the number 9**:

   $$(9 \times 9 =) 81 (8 \times 8 =) 64 (7 \times 7 =) 49 (6 \times 6 =) 36$$

   According to this pattern, the next term in this sequence is (5 x 5 =) **25**.

10. This number sequence is formed of **two alternating series**. In the first series: 128, 120, 32, 124, 8, 128, the next term is obtained by **dividing by 4 each time**:

   $$128 (\div 4 =) 32 (\div 4 =) 8$$

   In the second series: 128, 120, 32, 124, 8, 128, the next term is obtained by **adding 4 each time**:

   $$120 (+ 4 =) 124 (+ 4 =) 128$$

   As the next term in the sequence belongs to the first series, the term will be 8 (÷ 4 =) **2**.

11. This number sequence is formed of **two alternating series**. In the first series: <u>10</u>, 6, <u>8</u>, 6, <u>7</u>, 6, <u>7</u>, 6, the next term is obtained by **following the pattern – 2, – 1, – 0**:

$$10 \, (- 2 =) \, 8 \, (- 1 =) \, 7 \, (- 0 =) \, 7$$

In the second series: 10, <u>6</u>, 8, <u>6</u>, 7, <u>6</u>, 7, <u>6</u>, the next term is obtained by **adding 0 each time**:

$$6 \, (+ 0 =) \, 6 \, (+ 0 =) \, 6 \, (+ 0 =) \, 6$$

As the next term in the sequence belongs to the first series, the term will be 7 (+ 1 =) <u>**8**</u>.

12. In the first two pairs, the following pattern is used to make the second word of each pair:

s h a m e ⇨ mesh   a r c a n e ⇨ near
3 4   1 2   3 4   1 2

The result of applying this pattern to the first word of the third pair is as follows:

i n f r a
3 4 1 2

The letters to be used, therefore, are **i, n, r, a** and need to be re-ordered as: **r, a, i, n** = <u>rain</u>.

13. In the first two pairs, the following pattern is used to make the second word of each pair:

t i l e ⇨ t<u>a</u>l<u>l</u>   b i l e ⇨ b<u>a</u>l<u>l</u>
1 3   1 3

The result of applying this pattern to the first word of the third pair is as follows:

m i l e
1   3

The letters to be used, therefore, are **m** and **l** and they are to be kept in this order. Additionally, each time, the second letter 'i' is replaced with an 'a' and the fourth letter 'e' is replaced with an 'l'. This makes the missing word of the third pair <u>**mall**</u>.

14. In the first two pairs, the following pattern is used to make the second word of each pair:

p r e e n ⇨ pen   d e a d e n ⇨ den
1   2 3   1   2 3

The result of applying this pattern to the first word of the third pair is as follows:

m a i d e n
1   2 3

The letters to be used, therefore, are **m, e, n,** and they are to be kept in this order – i.e. <u>**men**</u>.

15. In the first two pairs, the following pattern is used to make the second word of each pair:

s l e d g i n g ⇨ leg   s w i n g e r s ⇨ wig
1 2   3   1 2   3

The result of applying this pattern to the first word of the third pair is as follows:

s t a g n a n t
1 2   3

The letters to be used, therefore, are **t, a, n** and they are to be kept in this order – i.e. <u>**tan**</u>.

16. In the first two pairs, the following pattern is used to make the second word of each pair:

t a m a r i n d ⇨ mat   t a s t e ⇨ sat
3 2   1   3 2 1

The result of applying this pattern to the first word of the third pair is as follows:

d e b a t e
3 2 1

The letters to be used, therefore, are **d, e, b** and need to be re-ordered as: **b, e, d** = <u>bed</u>.

17. This is a **complex code** which is obtained by moving the letters of the word using the sequence **– 3, – 2, – 1, + 0, + 1, + 2**. Hence, to de-code **JGMCFF**, the encoding pattern is reversed in the following way: **J + 3 places = M; G + 2 places = I; M + 1 place = N; C – 0 places = C; F – 1 place = E; F – 2 places = D**. The code **JGMCFF**, therefore, stands for the word <u>**MINCED**</u>.

18. This is a **complex code** which is obtained by moving the letters of the word using the sequence **+ 1, + 2, + 3, + 4, + 5**. Hence, to de-code **TMLVY**, the encoding pattern is reversed in the following way: **T – 1 place = S; M – 2 places = K;**

L – 3 places = I; V – 4 places = R; Y – 5 places = T. The code **TMLVY**, therefore, stands for the word <u>**SKIRT**</u>.

19.	This is a **complex code** which is obtained by moving the letters of the word using the sequence **+ 0, + 5, + 0, + 5, + 0**. Hence, the code for PLATE is found in the following way: **P + 0 places = P; L + 5 places = Q; A + 0 places = A; T + 5 places = Y; E + 0 places = E**. The code for **PLATE** is, therefore, <u>**PQAYE**</u>.
20.	This is a **mirror code** where each letter and its code are equal distances from the middle of the alphabet (i.e. the space between M and N). Hence, the code for FADED is found in the following way: **the mirror reflection of F = U; the mirror reflection of A = Z; the mirror reflection of D = W; the mirror reflection of E = V; the mirror reflection of D = W**. The code for **FADED** is, therefore, <u>**UZWVW**</u>.
21.	This is a **simple code** where each letter and its code are as follows: W is encoded as A; O is encoded as C; L is encoded as N; F is encoded as K. Hence, the code for FOWL is found in the following way: **F is encoded as K; O is encoded as C; W is encoded as A; L is encoded as N**. The code for **FOWL** is, therefore, <u>**KCAN**</u>.
22.	Adding <u>m</u> to the given letter clusters results in the following words: **album maroon totem mitten**. The letters b, d, k, and s can be used to complete some, but not all four, of the letter clusters.
23.	Adding <u>r</u> to the given letter clusters results in the following words: **liver revel chair robin**. The letters b, d, l, n, and s can be used to complete some, but not all four, of the letter clusters.
24.	Adding <u>o</u> to the given letter clusters results in the following words: **ditto oyster tango octave**. The letters a and y can be used to complete some, but not all four, of the letter clusters.
25.	Adding <u>g</u> to the given letter clusters results in the following words: **shrug gruel sting gouge**. The letters b, c, k, r, and t can be used to complete some, but not all four, of the letter clusters.
26.	Adding <u>s</u> to the given letter clusters results in the following words: **assess scythe stress staunch**. No other letters can be used to complete any of the letter clusters to form proper words.
27.	<u>**Chew**</u> and <u>**bite**</u> are the odd ones out because they **are verbs which mean to eat using one's teeth**, whereas drink, sip, and gulp are verbs which mean to swallow a liquid.
28.	<u>**Minority**</u> and <u>**handful**</u> are the odd ones out because they **are synonymous nouns meaning a few or a small amount**, whereas majority, mass, and bulk are synonymous nouns meaning a lot or a large amount.
29.	<u>**Wing**</u> and <u>**leg**</u> are the odd ones out because they **are body parts of living organisms**, whereas peel, fur, and skin are all types of outer layers or surfaces of living organisms.
30.	<u>**And**</u> and <u>**so**</u> are the odd ones out because they **are conjunctions**, whereas over, under, and below are prepositions.
31.	<u>**Dragon**</u> and <u>**gryphon**</u> are the odd ones out because they **are mythological creatures**, whereas witch, sorcerer, and warlock are human beings who supposedly possess magical powers.
32.	A comparison of all four given words reveals that only two words begin with the letter B (i.e. BOAR and BADE) and that two of the given numbers begin with 4, so **B = 4**. Therefore: • The code for BOAR must be either 4512 or 4356 • The code for BADE must be either 4512 or 4356 A closer comparison of BOAR and BADE reveals they have only one other letter in common: A, and, that the two possible codes only have one further digit in common: 5. Therefore, **A = 5**. Hence, we can deduce that **the code for BOAR is** <u>4356</u>.
33.	As we know the code for BOAR is 4356 (i.e. B = 4; O = 3; A = 5; R = 6), **the code for BADE must be 4512**. Therefore: **D = 1; E = 2**. Hence, **by substitution**, we can work out that **the code for BARE is** <u>4562</u>.
34.	As we know R = 6; A = 5; B = 4, we can deduce that **the last remaining code 7654 is the code for GRAB**. Therefore, **7 = G**. Now we have all the codes, **by substitution**, we can work out that **6572 is the code for** <u>RAGE</u>.
35.	As we know all the codes for all the letters, **by substitution**, we can work out that **7362 is the code for** <u>GORE</u>.
36.	A comparison of all the words reveals that three of them begin with the letter S (i.e. SEATS, STEMS, and STEAM). Similarly, a comparison of all the given sets of symbols reveals that two of them begin an *. Therefore, * **must be the symbol for S**. Consequently: • * ? £ ! * must be the set of symbols for either SEATS or STEMS (as these are the only two words that begin and end with an S) • * ? £ + ! must be the set of symbols for the word STEAM Therefore: **S is *; T is ?; E is £; A is +; M is !**. Hence, **through partial substitution**, we can deduce that the remaining set of symbols + * ? - $ stands for the word <u>ASTIR</u>.
37.	As we know S is *; T is ?; E is £; M is !, **by substitution**, we can deduce that * ? £ ! * stands for the word <u>STEMS</u>.
38.	As we know S is *; T is ?; E is £; A is +, **by substitution**, we can deduce that ? + * ? £ stands for the word <u>TASTE</u>.
39.	As we know the symbols for the all the letters, **by substitution**, we can deduce that * ? £ + ! stands for the word

40. Using the given information, we can deduce the following:

A. Harris and Calum are brothers ⇨ might be true. We are not told whether any of the children are related or not.

B. Lucy is always later than Tilly ⇨ might be true. It would be true if we knew that Lucy walked to school every day; however, we do not know this for certain.

C. Jimmy lives closer to the school than Tilly ⇨ might be true. We do not know how close either Jimmy or Tilly lives to the school. We also do not know how long it takes Jimmy to get to school on his scooter; all we know is that he gets to school in less than 10 minutes and that Tilly gets to school 4 minutes before Lucy (which is also less than 10 minutes).

D. Calum always arrives before Jimmy ⇨ **must be true. We are clearly told that Calum (and Harris) get to school by bike before Jimmy every day.**

E. Lucy always walks to school ⇨ might be true. While we are told how long it takes Lucy to get to school on foot, we do not know if she always walks to school.

41. To see the numerical problem, we substitute the letters for their given values:

$$A \times B \div E - D \quad \Rightarrow \quad 8 \times 12 \div 6 - 4$$

By carrying out the mathematical operations in stages, we arrive at the numerical answer of the problem:

$$8 \times 12 = 96 \quad 96 \div 6 = 16 \quad 16 - 4 = \mathbf{12}$$

As the number 12 is represented by the letter B, the answer is **B**.

42. To see the numerical problem, we substitute the letters for their given values:

$$E - D \times C \div A \quad \Rightarrow \quad 18 - 12 \times 6 \div 3$$

By carrying out the mathematical operations in stages, we arrive at the numerical answer of the problem:

$$18 - 12 = 6 \quad 6 \times 6 = 36 \quad 36 \div 3 = \mathbf{12}$$

As the number 12 is represented by the letter D, the answer is **D**.

43. To see the numerical problem, we substitute the letters for their given values:

$$(C^2 - B) \div D \quad \Rightarrow \quad (6^2 - 4) \div 8$$

By carrying out the mathematical operations in stages, we arrive at the numerical answer of the problem:

$$(6^2 - 4) = (36 - 4) \quad (36 - 4) = 32 \quad 32 \div 8 = \mathbf{4}$$

As the number 4 is represented by the letter B, the answer is **B**.

44. To see the numerical problem, we substitute the letters for their given values:

$$C \times D \div E + A \quad \Rightarrow \quad 18 \times 6 \div 12 + 3$$

By carrying out the mathematical operations in stages, we arrive at the numerical answer of the problem:

$$18 \times 6 = 108 \quad 108 \div 12 = 9 \quad 9 + 3 = \mathbf{12}$$

As the number 12 is represented by the letter E, the answer is **E**.

45. To see the numerical problem, we substitute the letters for their given values:

$$(4B + BC) \div D \quad \Rightarrow \quad (4 \times 4 + 4 \times 5) \div 6$$

By carrying out the mathematical operations in stages, we arrive at the numerical answer of the problem:

$$(4 \times 4 + 4 \times 5) = (16 + 4 \times 5) \quad (16 + 4 \times 5) = (16 + 20) \quad (16 + 20) = 36 \quad 36 \div 6 = \mathbf{6}$$

As the number 6 is represented by the letter D, the answer is **D**.

46. To see the numerical problem, we substitute the letters for their given values:

$$5(B + C) - 6D \quad \Rightarrow \quad 5 \times (2 + 3) - (6 \times 4)$$

By carrying out the mathematical operations in stages, we arrive at the numerical answer of the problem:

$$5 \times (2 + 3) = 5 \times (5) \quad 5 \times (5) = 25 \quad 25 - (6 \times 4) = 25 - (24) \quad 25 - 24 = \mathbf{1}$$

As the number 1 is represented by the letter A, the answer is **A**.

47. The completed word in the sentence should read as follows: The king entered the hall amidst a **FANFARE** of trumpets. Although the three-letter word PRO could be used to form the word PROFANE, the sentence would not make sense.

48. The completed word in the sentence should read as follows: Pleased with himself, Tony **SWAGGERED** into the room. Although the three-letter word TAG could be used to form the word STAGGERED, the sentence would not make sense.

49. The completed word in the sentence should read as follows: The wall was covered with colourful **GRAFFITI**.

50. The completed word in the sentence should read as follows: "I have a **WARRANT** for your arrest!" yelled the policeman. The following three-letter words could be used to complete RANT: CUR (CURRANT); OPE (OPERANT);

AMP (RAMPANT); KES (RANKEST), however, none of these words complete the sentence correctly.

51. The completed word in the sentence should read as follows: As the weather was nice, we had lunch on the **TERRACE**.

52. The analogy common to both pairs is that of **sources of materials**. <u>Gold</u> is extracted from a **mine**; <u>water</u> is extracted from a **well**.

53. The analogy common to both pairs is that of **aspects of natural phenomena**. We speak of a <u>flash</u> of **lightning** and of a <u>rumble</u> of **thunder**.

54. The analogy common to both pairs is that of **parallel letter changes**. <u>Flight</u> is the word **fight with the letter 'l' inserted after the initial letter 'f'**; <u>slight</u> is the word **sight with the letter 'l' inserted after the initial letter 's'**.

55. The analogy common to both pairs is that of **comparative forms of adjectives**. <u>Worse</u> is the comparative form of the adjective **bad** and <u>better</u> is the comparative form of the adjective **good**.

56. The analogy common to both pairs is that of **the homes of types of rabbits**. A **hutch** is where a <u>tame</u> rabbit lives and a **burrow** is where a <u>wild</u> rabbit lives.

57. Each time, the square roots of the first and third numbers are found; then the results of both operations are added together to obtain the second number:
9 (5) 4 ⇨ √9 = 3; √4 = 2; 3 + 2 = 5 ● 16 (9) 25 ⇨ √16 = 4; √25 = 5; 4 + 5 = 9 ● 4 (?) 36 ⇨ √4 = 2; √36 = 6; 2 + 6 = <u>**8**</u>

58. Each time, the third number is subtracted from the first number; then the result of the operation is squared to obtain the second number:
17 (9) 14 ⇨ 17 − 14 = 3; 3^2 = 9 ● 20 (36) 14 ⇨ 20 − 14 = 6; 6^2 = 36 ● 10 (?) 8 ⇨ 10 − 8 = 2; 2^2 = <u>**4**</u>

59. Each time, the first and third numbers are both divided by 4; then the results of the two division operations are added together to obtain the second number:
8 (11) 36 ⇨ 8 ÷ 4 = 2; 36 ÷ 4 = 9; 2 + 9 = 11 ● 16 (9) 20 ⇨ 16 ÷ 4 = 4; 20 ÷ 4 = 5; 4 + 5 = 9 ●
12 (?) 24 ⇨ 12 ÷ 4 = 3; 24 ÷ 4 = 6; 3 + 6 = <u>9</u>

60. Each time, the first and third numbers are added together; then their sum is multiplied by 3 to obtain the second number:
5 (42) 9 ⇨ 5 + 9 = 14; 14 x 3 = 42 ● 13 (78) 13 ⇨ 13 + 13 = 26; 26 x 3 = 78 ● **6 (?) 9 ⇨ 6 + 9 + 15; 15 x 3 = <u>45</u>**

61. Each time, the first and third numbers are multiplied by each other; then 2 is subtracted from their product to obtain the second number:
11 (20) 2 ⇨ 11 x 2 = 22; 22 − 2 = 20 ● 3 (19) 7 ⇨ 3 x 7 = 21; 21 − 2 = 19 ● **3 (?) 2 ⇨ 3 x 2 = 6; 6 − 2 = <u>4</u>**

62. The two words most opposite in meaning in the two given sets are <u>**obese (adj.)**</u> and <u>**thin (adj.)**</u>.
   - *Obese (adj.) is* to be extremely overweight, often to the point where it can be life-threatening.
   - *Thin (adj.) is* to be lean, i.e. not having excess fat or weight.

63. The two words most opposite in meaning in the two given sets are <u>**fake (adj.)**</u> and <u>**real (adj.)**</u>.
   - *Fake (adj.) is* being someone who, or something that, is not genuine.
   - *Real (adj.) is* being someone who, or something that, is genuine.

64. The two words most opposite in meaning in the two given sets are <u>**sow (v.)**</u> and <u>**harvest (v.)**</u>.
   - *Sow (v.) is* to plant seeds (i.e. to place seeds in the ground in order for them to grow into plants, trees, etc.).
   - *Harvest (v.) is* to collect ripe plants or crops etc. from the place they have grown.

65. The two words most opposite in meaning in the two given sets are <u>**heartfelt (adj.)**</u> and <u>**insincere (adj.)**</u>.
   - *Heartfelt (adj.) is* being sincere or deeply felt.
   - *Insincere (adj.) is* lacking or not having sincerity; being false or hypocritical.

66. The two words most opposite in meaning in the two given sets are <u>**behind (prep.)**</u> and <u>**before (prep.)**</u>.
   - *Behind (prep.) is* used to indicate a place or position at, or towards, the back of someone or something.
   - *Before (prep.) is* used to indicate a place or position in front of, or ahead of, someone or something.

67. The first set of words is governed by the following rule:

c e l l <u>o</u> (l o c k) <u>k</u> n i g h t
<u>3</u>   1 2   1 2 3 4 <u>4</u>

By applying this rule to the second set of words we can see the following:

<u>m</u> o l <u>a r</u> (?) <u>s</u> l i g h t
<u>3</u>   1 2   <u>4</u>

The letters to be used, therefore, are **m, a, r, s** and need to be re-ordered as: **a, r, m, s = <u>arms</u>**.

68. The first set of words is governed by the following rule:

a r r o w (r o a d) c l o d
3 1   2   1 2 3 4   4

By applying this rule to the second set of words we can see the following:

u s i n g (?) p l u g
3 1 2   4

The letters to be used, therefore, are **u, s, n, g** and need to be re-ordered as: **s, n, u, g = snug**.

69. The first set of words is governed by the following rule:

m e d i u m (m u s t) a s t e r n
        2 1   1 2 3 4   3 4

By applying this rule to the second set of words we can see the following:

a b s o r b (?) p a n d e r
        2 1   3 4

The letters to be used, therefore, are **r, b, a, n** and need to be re-ordered as: **b, r, a, n = bran**.

70. The first set of words is governed by the following rule:

o d o u r (p l o d) p a l l s
  4 3   1 2 3 4   1   2

By applying this rule to the second set of words we can see the following:

m e d i c (?) h e l i x
  4 3   1   2

The letters to be used, therefore, are **e, d, h, i** and need to be re-ordered as: **h, i, d, e = hide**.

71. The first set of words is governed by the following rule:

u p p e r (p u l l) c a l l s
2   1   1 2 3 4   3 4

By applying this rule to the second set of words we can see the following:

a n g e r (?) m a t e r
2   1   3 4

The letters to be used, therefore, are **a, g, t, e** and need to be re-ordered as: **g, a, t, e = gate**.

72. To find the missing letter pair, **P moves + 3 places to S and T moves + 2 places to V** ⇨ **SV**.

73. To find the missing letter pair, **X is mirrored to obtain C; W is mirrored to obtain D; the resultant mirror pair CD is then inverted to obtain DC** ⇨ **DC**.

74. To find the missing letter pair, **K is mirrored to obtain P and E is mirrored to obtain V** ⇨ **PV**.

75. To find the missing letter pair, **KP is a mirror pair (K is the mirror of P); K moves – 2 places to I; I is then mirrored to obtain R** ⇨ **IR**.

76. To find the missing letter pair, **A is mirrored to obtain Z; E is mirrored to obtain V; the resultant mirror pair ZV is then inverted to obtain VZ** ⇨ **VZ**.

77. The only two words that form a proper word when combined are **bed** and **rock** to give **bedrock**.

78. The only two words that form a proper word when combined are **partner** and **ship** to give **partnership**. Pasnip (pa + snip) is an incorrect spelling of 'parsnip'.

79. The only two words that form a proper word when combined are **on** and **us** to give **onus**. Init (in + it) is an incorrect spelling of 'innit'.

80. The only two words that form a proper word when combined are **col** and **our** to give **colour**. Hilllock (hill + lock) is an incorrect spelling of 'hillock' and collour (col + lour) is an incorrect spelling of 'colour'.

GLOSSARY

The numbers in brackets after each definition refer to the Test and question number where the glossed word is found. For example, (3.43) means that the glossed word is found in Practice Test Paper 3, Question 43.

Adjust (v.) is to change oneself or an item to fit or suit a particular situation or purpose. (2.48)

Album (n.) is a book of blank pages that is used to hold collections of items such as stamps, photographs, etc. (3.22)

Bawl (v.) is to cry, or to shout, very loudly. (2.72)

Bedrock (n.) is the basis or foundation of something (e.g. an idea, a philosophy, an attitude, an approach, etc.). (3.77)

Cardigan (n.) is a knitted jacket with sleeves that is buttoned down the front. (2.73)

Clover (n.) is a plant that belongs to the pea family and is often used as fodder for cattle. (1.8)

Col (n.) is, in geology, the lowest point between two mountain peaks and usually provides a path or pass from one side of a mountain range to another. (3.80)

Din (n.) is a loud, unpleasant noise (usually one that goes on for a long time). (1.6)

Ditto (n.) is a noun which means the same thing; the same as what is above; the same as what has just been said. (3.24)

Emit (v.) is to give out something (e.g. light, a smell, heat, etc.). (1.77)

Fanfare (n.) is a short piece of music (generally played on trumpets) to announce or introduce an important arrival or event. (3.47)

Furbelow (n.) is a type of dress trimming that is often made up of pleats or material that is gathered in a pleat-like way. (2.77)

Gouge (v.) is to cut something out with, or as if you had used, a tool that resembles a corer (a piece of kitchen equipment used to remove the cores of fruit and vegetables like apples and courgettes). (3.25)

Graffiti (n.) is a plural noun used to refer to the drawings or words that are painted or sprayed onto public surfaces (e.g. walls of buildings, bridges, etc.). (3.49)

Gruel (n.) is a kind of porridge that is thin (i.e. not thick and gloopy). (3.25)

Hake (n.) is a type of sea-fish. (1.3)

Hillock (n.) is a small hill. (3.80)

Kin (n.) is people who belong to the same family; a person's relatives. (1.1)

Liver (n.) is an important organ found in humans and other vertebrates which carries out many functions related to digestion, the blood, etc. (3.23)

Lour (v.) is to scowl; to look angry. (3.80)

Maggot (n.) is the worm-like larva of different types of flies. (2.71)

Maroon (n.) is a colour that is a dark brownish-red or a dark purplish-red. (3.22)

Merge (v.) is to combine, join, or mix at least two things. (2.36)

Mitten (n.) is a type of glove (often woolly) that is divided into two sections only: one for the thumb and one for the four fingers. (3.22)

Nag (n.) is a horse, usually one which is old and broken-down. (1.1)

Octave (n.) is 1. a group of eight things. 2. in music, a series of notes that lies between the first and eighth notes of a scale (either major or minor). 3. in poetry, a stanza or verse that is made up of eight lines. (3.24)

Omen (n.) is an event or thing that is seen as a sign of something happening in the future which could be good or evil. (1.9)

Onus (n.) is a burden or responsibility. (3.79)

Oyster (n.) is a common name for clams or molluscs (which are marine creatures). (3.24)

Partnership (n.) is a relationship between two or more people who work together as partners (i.e. people who are on an equal footing with one another), often in a commercial business, but by no means exclusively so. (3.78)

Purée (n.) is, in cooking, an amount of foodstuffs (e.g. vegetables, fruit, meat, etc.) that has been reduced to smooth pulp, either by straining the foodstuffs through a sieve, or by using a liquidizer. (1.10)

Ream (n.) is 500 sheets of paper. (1.6)

Revel (n.) is lively, noisy merrymaking. (3.23)

Scythe (n.) is a tool with a handle and large curved blade that is used to cut crops or grass by hand. (3.26)

Staggered (v.) is the past simple form of the verb 'to stagger' which is to walk or to move unsteadily. (3.48)

Staunch (v.) is to stop the flow of something (often, but not always, a liquid such as blood). (3.26)

Swaggered (v.) is the past simple form of the verb 'to swagger' which is 1. to walk in a pompous manner. 2. to behave in an arrogant fashion. (3.48)

Tango (n.) is a Latin-American dance. (3.24)

Terrace (n.) is a level area by the side of a house that is paved and raised. (3.51)

Totem (n.) is, in the culture of Native Americans, an object from the natural world, often an animal, which is used as a symbol or sign of a tribe or of a person. (3.22)

Warrant (n.) is a legal document that gives the person who possesses it the authority to carry out certain activities. (3.50)

Woe (n.) is intense sadness or sorrow. (2.34)

Made in the USA
Las Vegas, NV
29 June 2021